Reflections on Artificial Intelligence

Blay Whitby

intellect™

First Published in 1996 by
Intellect Books
EFAE, Earl Richards Road North, Exeter EX2 6AS

Consulting editor: Masoud Yazdani
Page layout: Robin Beecroft

A catalogue record for this book is available from the British Library

ISBN 1-871516-68-4

Printed and bound in Great Britain by Cromwell Press, Wiltshire

Contents

Acknowledgements

It is, of course, impossible for me to remember all the people who have directly contributed to the ideas in this book; so many friends and colleagues have freely given time to discuss issues or comment on early drafts. I am particularly indebted to Margaret Boden, Ron Chrisley, Kyran Dale, Joe Faith, Pat Hayes, Inman Harvey, Phil Jones, Brian Keeley, Bill Keller, Ajit Narayanan, Tim Passingham, Donald Peterson, Mike Sharples, Aaron Sloman, Steve Torrance, Sharon Wood, and Masoud Yazdani.

I also want to thank Robin Beecroft and Nick Szczepanik for their help in turning a collection of ideas into something resembling a book.

For my parents

Preface

Few subjects are so misrepresented in print as the social implications of Artificial Intelligence (AI). AI enthusiasts, and their critics, gain far more attention in the media by raising the spectre of the almost imminent appearance of human-surpassing robots[1]. This spectre has done nothing but harm to AI. Not only does it present a misleading picture of where technological developments are leading, it also distracts public attention from the real social implications of technology that is already being introduced.

There are many reasons for this misrepresentation. A sensational account will almost always get more publicity than a more sober one. Much of this book pours scorn upon the so called 'threat' of human-surpassing robots. The technical assumptions behind the threat are simplistic; there are no good reasons to assume that progress in AI is likely to achieve anything like this in the foreseeable future. However, the fundamental mistake behind this sort of claim lies in the almost total ignorance of social dynamics in those who make it. A moment's reflection should be enough to reveal that in human history there has been little, if any, correlation between high intelligence and authority. A further moment should be enough to reveal that humans have little desire for such a correlation. This gives two good reasons to doubt that, even in the (as yet unlikely) situation that we were to build artifacts that surpassed us in certain types of intellectual prowess, they would thereby automatically acquire some sort of authority over us or pose any sort of threat.

In the case of AI, there are also unfortunate psychological forces at work. Just as humans were reluctant to abandon the view of themselves as at the centre of the universe, so they remain unwilling to accept that intelligence could function in very un-humanlike ways. It has always been easier for the public and science fiction writers to portray AI as about to produce artificial humans. This portrayal has been helped by the influence of the Turing test, which now needs to be re-examined. Significantly, we also have a wide range of skills and experience in relating to human beings. It is, therefore, easier to imagine relating to AI as if it were human. It is only too easy for humans mistakenly to project onto AI their distrust of highly intelligent humans. Or because they are strongly motivated to achieve power over other humans to assume that intelligent artifacts would, obviously, share the same motivation. The reality, of course, is less sensational and much more complex.

In a similar fashion, most works on the philosophical implications of AI concentrate on the contribution AI has made and will make to the philosophy of mind. There is a great deal of philosophical interest in the way in which AI interacts with such established philosophical positions as dualism, behaviourism, functionalism, and the mystery of consciousness. This book attempts to avoid these debates as far as possible. They are undoubtedly interesting questions, but a distraction from the motivation of this book - to provide a clear basis for the discussion of the social implications of AI. Indeed they add to the problems of anthropocentricity briefly alluded to above.

The main real technological achievement of AI has been the entire field of computation. Computer science is historically a sub-field of AI. It is also true to say that computation is a part of human intelligent activity which AI has succeeded in reproducing artificially. The public have come to accept computation as including calculation, and the handling of large quantities of information. They now need to adjust to the notion of computers giving expert advice in various areas. The social implications of this should be fairly obvious - who is checking on the sort of advice given, what presuppositions guide the design and introduction of these systems, and is someone or some organisation avoiding responsibility by hiding behind the AI system?

The development of AI is not stopping at advice-giving systems. The new technological developments including neural nets and evolved devices (collectively called 'nouvelle AI') are more difficult to predict and monitor than previous more algorithmic methods. As is frequently claimed in the following pages, AI should not be seen as a stand-alone technology. It has been, and will continue to be, incorporated in all sorts of other technologies. This makes scrutiny of its social implications much more difficult yet even more important. However, it also holds out interesting new possibilities. The difficulties for humans in monitoring nouvelle AI might be ameliorated by using earlier AI techniques to do the monitoring. Such systems have yet to appear, but there is some urgency to this task.

This book is not about new technologies, nor about social change, though it has important things to say on both subjects. Its central subject is the influence of powerful ideas. Powerful ideas are those ideas which reshape our lives. For many centuries such ideas have come from religion and the arts; nowadays they are coming mainly from science and technology. The conviction which drives me to write is that, whatever the source of powerful ideas, they need to be discussed as widely as possible.

This conviction is backed by one which some may find more controversial: namely that social change is not an inevitable or impersonal process. It is rather a collection of human choices. At every one of those choice points an individual or collection of individuals could have chosen otherwise. It therefore behoves decision-makers to be as informed as possible with respect to novel possibilities. Only then can we be certain that optimal choices are made.

Who are the decision-makers? In this case we all are. Almost every human takes some decisions which will shape the impact of technology on our lives. Perhaps they do so in choosing to work in one industry rather than another. Perhaps they do so in choosing to spend a little more money on a video recorder which has (or is claimed to have) an artificial intelligence component. More often they do so simply by not bothering to examine the choices of those who choose for them.

It is therefore cause for surprise and dismay that many, if not most, of the questions raised by the future course of scientific and technological development are rarely discussed in a balanced way. This book can raise only a small number of the issues concerned, and attempt to do so in a balanced rather than sensational way. Its intention is merely to provide a starting point for discussion.

This is a multi-disciplinary book. Within these various disciplines there are differing conventions and styles. In addition, authorities recognized as central within one discipline may be unknown in some others. Since there is no single style which would be appropriate for lawyers, computer scientists, and philosophers, for example, I have attempted simply to be clear. I hope that this intention requires no apology. I do, however, apologize for many brief ventures into different subject areas in which I am not expert. Often these will appear, to those readers knowledgeable in that area, insufficiently technical in style.

Similar problems exist with references. It would have been impractical to attempt to cite the relevant authorities in every related discipline. A parsimonious approach has therefore been adopted, giving precedence to those authorities who seem to straddle or cross disciplinary boundaries. This should not, at least without further evidence, be taken as implying any ignorance on my part. It is to be hoped that sufficient references exist to enable the interested reader to pursue topics further.

None of this should be taken as implying that any multi-disciplinary expertise is required on the part of the reader. Just because the book includes references to connectionsim, catharsis, and constitutional theory does not imply that the reader need be expert in all or any of these areas. Since I regard disciplinary boundaries as nothing more than administrative inconveniences, I encourage the reader to do likewise. Interest in the subject matter should be sufficient to ensure understanding.

The primary purpose of the book is to start debate on an area that, for reasons mentioned above, and a whole range of others, is all too often neglected. Another year or two would have produced a more thorough volume, but the issues are urgent.

Note

1. A claim made recently by both Hans Moravec and Kevin Warwick (Future Fantastic, BBC 1, 28.6.96).

Introduction: New Science, New Technologies and Society

When people discuss the influence of technology upon society they tend to have a nineteenth-century picture of this influence. They tend to look for machines like steam engines: spectacular, noisy and, to varying degrees, physically dangerous. In terms of the social implications, they are generally concerned about issues such as mass unemployment, changing patterns of work, privacy, and security.

The new technology of the late twentieth century is rather different. The microprocessors that have found their way under the bonnets of cars and into washing machines are silent and unseen. The less tangible effects of new technologies and contemporary science are often neglected. These include the way in which they raise new ideas, new possibilities and new ways of looking at humanity and society.

This distinction is particularly important with respect to Artificial Intelligence (AI). AI has not produced as much in obvious technology as has sometimes been hoped for or predicted. It has most obviously not produced the hordes of spectacular and dangerous robots predicted by science fiction. Similar remarks apply to the social implications of AI: its direct influence on employment patterns, for example, can realistically be described as negligible. This claim is defended in detail in Chapter 2.

On the other hand, the influence of AI on ways of looking at society and the question of what it is to be human has been out of all proportion to the amount of working technology it has so far delivered. This is particularly true of psychology, where cognitive science is channeling AI-derived ideas of the nature of mind into current scientific thinking about the human mind. It is also true of philosophy, where AI-derived ideas have caused controversy that is in no sense related to the relatively small amount of AI technology experienced by the general public.

Although it might be argued that philosophy and psychology have very few (if any) social implications, it is reasonable to assume that, in the near future, ideas from these academic disciplines will spread into society. This in turn will generate the social implications with which we should be concerned. AI is a technology that is, perhaps more than any other, adept at the production of powerful ideas. This is probably because the nature of human intelligence and deep questions about what it is to be human (or for that matter, non-human in human society) can never be totally excluded from any discussion of AI.

A central theme of this book is that the influence of new technologies through the generation of powerful ideas affects society at large, as well as the more academic pursuits mentioned above. One consequence of this is that we cannot delay debate of the social implications of new technologies. If we wait until there are many examples of technologies such as AI or virtual reality (VR) in general use, we will simply be too late to discuss the important social implications of these technologies. This cannot be overemphasised. One finds little enthusiasm for debating the social implications of new technologies at an early stage. Those concerned with the development of the technology are understandably enthused by the ideas with which they are working and see social implications as a (premature) distraction. Those more interested in social issues see the technology in simplistic terms and are generally unwilling to criticise the ideas emerging from a particular research paradigm separately from the paradigm itself. In the case of AI, which has historically tended to generate more in the way of influential ideas than effective technology, it is simply false that debate of the social consequences can be delayed until it is in more widespread use. Subsequent chapters provide several examples.

Similar remarks apply to the methodological assumptions of the scientists who perform the research that makes this new technology possible. Here the contrast with nineteenth century science could not be more spectacular. Nineteenth century science had a great deal of influence at the level of powerful ideas. Its view of the universe as fundamentally predictable and deterministic suggested that humans and their societies must be similar sorts of machines. The rigid and deterministic nature of nineteenth century machinery suggested rigid and deterministic views of human nature and of society. Large-scale and rigid automated organizations naturally followed.

The methodological assumptions of modern science are completely different. This sort of determinism has been left behind. We now live in a universe that is fundamentally indeterminate and, in many aspects, governed by the mathematics of chaos. Prediction is, at best, only occasionally possible and within strict limits. Modern 'machines' are very different from their nineteenth century counterparts. The sort of machines with which modern sciences such as AI are concerned can realistically be described as having 'goals' or 'purposes' and as containing 'knowledge'. This is a feature of AI that has been eloquently described (Boden 1978, Turkle 1984) and has many exciting consequences, but has yet to filter into the public notion of a machine. When it does, we can expect widespread changes in social organisations.

In spite of the unfortunate persistence of some nineteenth century views of the way in which a machine works, AI research indirectly, but importantly, influences scientific views of the nature of such things as mind, humanity, and society. These ideas are beginning to have important social consequences. Many examples of this influence are discussed in subsequent chapters.

Some Examples of the Influence of AI on Society

One area that is discussed in detail in this collection is the influence of AI upon legal and judicial thinking. This discussion is not focussed upon the increasing use of AI to give legal judgements or to support legal professionals in decision making, though these are certainly important areas. It is, rather, focussed upon the way in which ideas from AI can have surprising social implications in the legal area. These include changing the constitutional balance of power between legislators and the judiciary. Another idea is the reduction in the importance of human judgement and discretion in the application of existing legislation. These may appear abstract and technical matters, but they are not. In terms of the effects of AI upon the way we will live in the future, they are infinitely more significant than discussing whether a few lawyers or legal secretaries will be made redundant by the introduction of legal expert systems.

One of the most important, and obvious, of these ideas is the suggestion that non-human agents (of which AI systems provide a prototype) might be increasingly involved in areas where we had previously believed that only human agents could participate. If this is possible (even in theory) then there is an urgent need to discuss the implications of this. Before the suggestion of such a possibility, this sort of discussion would have been unnecessary. This is discussed in greater detail below and in Chapter 4.

Even when considering working technology, the social implications of AI may be more at the level of changing ideas than at the level of unemployment and physical danger. For example, one highly suitable application area for AI has been observed by Feigenbaum (Feigenbaum 1993). He suggests that there will be a growing use of AI to produce rule-following systems or rule-helpers. Such systems would advise or check on compliance with complex legal or administrative systems. Systems of this sort have already been introduced and form the basis of what is likely to be a major application area for AI.

The social implications of this sort of application are complex, but illustrative of the theme of this book. This seems an ideal application area for AI. Such systems can be built with existing technology and AI techniques. The results are almost certain to be clearer, quicker decisions on matters such as entitlement to welfare payments, tax deductions, and similar matters. There are no direct dangers posed by such systems, provided they are designed and maintained in a professional manner (see Whitby 1988 for an examination of what this might entail). Even if they are highly imperfect, they offer a usually beneficial application of AI for both the administrators and the public.

The danger lies in the sort of processes that quite probably will be set in train by the introduction of such systems. The widespread availability of rule-helper systems will certainly remove any incentive for legislators and administrators to simplify or clarify the rules they seek to impose. It is also likely that legislators and administrators will increase rules and regulations to take advantage of the existing of 'rule helper' systems. This may be to the ultimate disadvantage of those who are bound by the rules. In the worst case, the rules may become so complex that only those with access to the latest AI technology have any hope of understanding them. Those who cannot afford this will be severely disadvantaged. Even in less extreme possible cases there may be a significant increase in costs and a greater reliance on technological assistance, rather than human interpretation.

On the other hand, if cheap and readily-available AI systems could help those who are already overwhelmed and possibly disadvantaged as a result of already existing complex laws and regulations, this would present a very different set of social implications. Note that the contrast between these scenarios does not depend on technological developments, but rather on who exploits the possibilities opened by the technology, and on the purposes for which it is exploited.

A related area to that of legal reasoning is that of moral reasoning. It is often remarked that a fundamental weakness of present AI systems in law is their lack of any 'sense of justice'. It quite possible that future developments of AI systems could lead, either accidentally or by design, to the inclusion of certain features that either comprise, or effectively simulate (depending on one's philosophical viewpoint), a sense of justice. This development has both reassuring and worrying features. It is reassuring in that it will make AI systems in law less blind to some of the important human principles that (in some rather complex sense) underlie the application of purely legal principles. It is worrying in that it raises many even more difficult questions. For example, if the human sense of justice turns out to be poorly structured, inconsistent and therefore difficult to reproduce in an artefact, should we replace it with a better structured more consistent version? This is a question that may well present itself as a purely technical decision for the designers of legal systems, yet which has wide-reaching social consequences.

Once again it suggests the introduction of a non-human agency to an area where we had previously only considered the possibility of human agency. We are familiar with the idea of humans carrying out reasoning in the area of what is just and what is not. Most people can discuss the nature of justice (although they might disagree strongly about what exactly it entails). AI raises the possibility, if nothing more, of an artefact carrying out this form of reasoning. There are many complex questions woven together here. Subsequent chapters attempt to disentangle some of them. They range from philosophical questions as to whether such a thing is possible, even in principle, through technical questions about how exactly it might be done, to social and moral questions about whether it ought to be done, and if so, when?

These questions involve many disciplines and are unlikely to yield clear-cut uncontroversial answers. This, however, can be no excuse for not attending to them. If they are neglected then technical developments may take place without the necessary reflection and we may come to lament a world in which quite preventable technological misery has been forced upon us, simply through neglect. One place in which this has already happened is mentioned in Chapter 10,'The Virtual Sky is not the Limit', on the ethics of VR. The observations show that neglect of the level of simulated violence encouraged by some contemporary computer games means that it will be very difficult to frame legislation to prevent VR being used as an extremely violent form of entertainment. With fast-developing technology, it is no good waiting for its widespread use and then attempting to decide exactly what limits we want to place on it.

Various divisions of attitudes to the social implications of AI have been proposed in recent years (see Whitby 1984, 1988). For the purposes of the present discussion it is perhaps best to use the division proposed by the Council for Science and Society (CSS 1989). Their division has the scientific merit of being based upon a survey of AI researchers carried out in 1987 by the US Office of Technology Assessment. They identify three clusters of attitudes towards the future development of AI. First, there are the Believers, who are strongly optimistic about the results of AI research. They see the social changes likely to be brought about by AI as mostly positive, but inevitable in any case. By contrast, the Disbelievers see many of the goals of AI research as not possible at all, or not possible in the way that they are framed by AI researchers. The third group, the Social Critics, hold the view that although AI may eventually succeed at many of its goals, the social implications will be largely negative.

These three clusters of attitudes form a basis for the discussion of the target groups on the implications of AI and are used in some of the following sections to help show the relationships between the issues discussed.

Finally, it is also important to note that the relationship between new technology and powerful ideas also works in the opposite direction. It is not the case that society is the passive recipient of the new ideas generated by those working in AI That is to say that the progress of technology is shaped as much by some of the ideas that are prevalent in a given society at a particular time as by technological possibilities. Once again this is a process that requires much discussion. Two chapters in particular: Chapter 6, 'Ethical AI', and Chapter 3,'Why The Turing test is AI's biggest blind alley', deal, in part, with the influence of social ideas on the technological development of AI.

Technological Positivism

One of the most significant of the ideas discussed (and strongly criticised) in the following chapters might be called 'technological positivism'. It is well worth investing some time exploring this idea in detail. Technological positivism is closely related to other forms of positivism[1] with the added contemporary appeal that it often claims support from the use of expensive, high-tech machinery. The technological positivist claims that to the extent that a process can be successfully reproduced by a machine, and in the absence of any further evidence, then the way in which that machine carries out the process is the optimal (sometimes even the only) way of carrying out that process. The idea of technological positivism pervades AI research so profoundly that critics of AI often mistakenly criticise technological positivism, rather than AI. When the defenders of AI then point out, quite correctly, that enthusiasm for AI research in no sense entails technological positivism, they risk appearing disingenuous.

Some examples should help to clarify the position of the technological positivist. It has long been a goal of AI to enable computers to understand natural language. It has also emerged that certain types of writing style are easier for computer programs to interpret than others. The conclusion that technological positivists draw from this, without any further evidence, is that those types of writing style that computers find more amenable are in some sense better than those that are computationally less tractable. They view human writing that proves difficult for a computer program to interpret as confused, poor style, logically unstructured or in some other way defective. In extreme cases it is even argued that the way to assess whether or not a piece of human writing is good or clear is to determine how well it can be assimilated by some particular computer program.

In this stark example the dangers of too freely adopting the approach of the technological positivist are apparent. There are many differing approaches to the assessment of what is good or clear writing. It is probably inevitable that there should not be universal agreement on such questions. The introduction of a (highly arbitrary) technological test contributes nothing to such debates. Indeed we may well suspect the technological positivists of using a computational 'Trojan Horse' to impose their own particular views of what constitutes good writing style on to this rich diversity.

If the example of the technological positivists' approach to writing style appears somewhat contrived and obvious, it may usefully be followed by an example that is certainly neither. Technological positivism is also dangerously prevalent in the field of AI and the law. It is sometimes argued,for example, that the task of encoding a piece of legislation in Prolog is a good test of its consistency and suitability for enactment. If technological positivism were pursued to its ultimate conclusion, it follows that we could in principle institute a mechanised test of legislation thay would help to remove inconsistent or vague laws. This too has been proposed. It is important to note that the 'Prolog test' of legislation is as irrelevant as the computational tractability test described in the last example. Indeed, Chapter 5., 'AI and the Law: Proceed with Caution', argues that the approach of what I am characterising as the technological positivist in the field of AI and the law either deliberately or unconsciously hides a shift in the relative power of legislature and judiciary in modern society. It is essential that this should be publicly debated in terms of a shift of power, and not only in terms of technological choices.

We may be concerned similarly about the inconsistencies in sentences handed out by human judges and magistrates. Technological positivism would tend automatically to view these inconsistencies as mistakes and suggest that it might be better to use a computer or similar system that could give far greater consistency. It is true that an AI system could be introduced that would give far greater consistency. What needs to be established is whether or not such an increase in consistency would be an improvement. This is a debate about what exactly we require from a legal system. The properties of technology, however exciting, should not be seen as the most important issues in such a debate. There are clear dangers in allowing technological positivists to dominate the debate on AI and the law.

An Overview of the Reflections

The implications of AI range over a very wide area and, reflecting an attempt to do likewise, the following chapters seem to touch on a wide variety of subjects. As has been remarked in the Preface, different readers will bring vastly different background knowledge and interests to what is a highly interdisciplinary field. Inevitably, some parts of the book will be more relevant to particular backgrounds and interests than to others. Nevertheless, there are many common themes that require outlining at this stage.

The first theme considers the nature of AI itself. There are many misconceptions about what AI is, even within the discipline. Indeed, for reasons that are explored in chapter 2, practitioners of AI often disagree about, and are sometimes guilty of spreading misconceptions about, the nature of the field. It is not surprising, therefore, that the public have many misconceptions about the nature of AI. I do not propose to give a definition of AI here (see Whitby 1988 for a full discussion), but rather to remark on some important features of AI which underly the discussions of its implications in this volume.

AI is not to be defined by its methods, so I am using the term to cover all the various historical methods which have been employed to build various sorts of intelligence into various sorts of artefacts and whatever future methods may be tried. I have no view as to the relative success quotients of any particular AI techniques. (There are differences between the social implications of various AI techniques and these are remarked upon where appropriate.)

It is also important to dispel some common public misconceptions about AI. For example, it is often believed that AI has either failed or will make a sudden breakthrough. Both these misconceptions are explored in the following chapters. Chapter 2, 'The Social Implications of AI' shows how repeated changes of fashion about AI techniques lead to unfair denigration of techniques that are not seen as the latest fashion. Chapter 3, 'Why the Turing test is AI's biggest blind alley', gives a more important explanation of why success in AI is often seen as an 'all or nothing' phenomenon. The Turing test is named after a thought experiment proposed by Alan Turing in 1950, and much discussed ever since. The influence of this thought experiment on the history of AI has been vast and for reasons discussed in Chapter 3 should now be seen as generally negative. It has contributed to the misconceptions about AI mentioned above by suggesting that AI is about more or less total reproduction of human intelligence.

It is also claimed that Turing's 1950 paper has been generally misinterpreted as containing an operational definition of intelligence. This misinterpretation has caused AI to be overly pre-occupied with imitating certain human abilities. This in turn has distracted AI research from the sort of approaches likely to produce useful products and interesting theories. In short, the attempt to directly imitate human abilities is a 'blind alley' as far as AI research is concerned.

A more accurate, and more useful, interpretation of Turing's paper is first, that it reflects a paradigm shift in the relationship between physical and logical properties, and second, that it makes an important point on the central role of human attitudes in determining the answers to questions such as: 'can machines think?'. Looking at Turing's 1950 paper in this way once again highlights the overlap between technical and social issues in AI. In this case, it is the reverse influence of social attitudes shaping technological development, as mentioned above. It is refreshing to re-examine one of the earliest pieces of AI philosophy in this way. As I have observed elsewhere (Whitby 1988), many AI developments have mistakenly focussed on replacing (rather than assisting) human beings. The long-standing misinterpretation of the Turing test may have played an important role in this.

If AI is not about this sort of wholesale mimicry or replacement of human abilities, then what would give a better picture? One approach that is taken up in Chapter 4,'AI and the Law: Learning to Speak each other's Language', namely the notion of 'creeping AI'. In many fields (and the Law is a paradigm example), the influence of AI will be slow but pervasive, rather than revolutionary. This means that ideas from AI will gradually become more prevalent in the legal sphere. The technological counterpart of this spread of ideas will be that humans will have to live and work surrounded by technology that becomes progressively smarter. This is different from the future suggested by the Turing test, and by some of the Believers in that there is no sudden change from machinery that is stupid to machinery which is intelligent. Instead there is a more gradual change, which is hard to describe in such terms.

There are a number of reasons to believe that this future is more likely to come about than one where human-like intelligence in artefacts suddenly becomes possible. First, and most important, this is the exact development which has taken place over the last 50 years. Modern computing and information technology is, despite widespread belief to the contrary, an offshoot of AI. It is historically the case that the quest for AI pre-dates modern computer technology and that the whole field of computing is a successful sub-field of AI. Before about 1945, the term computing referred to a purely human activity, today it would normally be assumed that it referred to an activity performed by artifacts of various sorts. People have grown accustomed to the idea that the various activities subsumed by the term computation can be performed better by machines than by humans, and through the second half of the twentieth century the list of such activities has gradually expanded. Routine copying, transmission, and checking of files is an area where human capacities have been generally exceeded. Certain types of medical diagnosis, mineral prospecting and chess playing provide more recent examples. There is every reason to believe that this process will continue, though not in a spectacular or Turing-test-like general way. Second, this process reflects a development that is market-driven rather than the consequence of wild speculation. There is a demand for improved 'smartness' (for want of a better word) in certain types of machinery in certain specialised areas. There is no obvious demand for a device that passes the Turing test. A cynical marketing expert might say that the planet was already overstocked with them.

There are further examples of the themes outlined above to be found by examining the interface between AI and the Law. In addition to various technical problems that have to be solved, there will be an interchange of ideas and methodologies. As in several other areas, the indirect influence of AI will be to prompt legal professionals to examine new methodologies and consider new possibilities.

One particular area already mentioned is the way in which the law will have to develop appropriate responses to the notion of non-human agents performing actions that have so far been performed only by human beings. This is a task for legal professionals rather than AI enthusiasts. In order to do this they need to take an active interest in the philosophical foundations of AI. It is important for them to be aware of the dangers of technological positivism. For the first time in legal history, it may be necessary to debate the marking out of certain tasks as activities for humans only; not because, as in the past, human performance on these tasks is the best available, but because humanity is considered important in and of itself. This debate is far from clear-cut. Many people, given a serious choice, may prefer to be tried by computer rather than by humans. What is important about this debate is that it concerns legal experts and human choices. It should not be abducted by Believers, or the Disbelievers for that matter. The philosophical ideas that guide the development of AI should not necessarily be absorbed into the legal area without criticism.

Influence will also take effect in the reverse direction. That is to say that in order to build systems that are useful to the legal profession, AI professionals will have to examine some of their most basic working assumptions. For example, legal applications may necessitate a re-examination of what McDermott has called the 'logicist' position in AI (McDermott 1987). In addition, debate has already started on the exact implications of the claim that the work of the legal profession is a rule-based activity.

Both directions of influence are claimed to be beneficial, in the long-term, both for AI research and the theory of jurisprudence. However, they also entail the conclusion that it will probably not be easy to build useful AI-based legal systems in the immediate future, though the technical possibilities are completely separate from the desirability of such developments.

Chapter 5, AI and the Law: Proceed with Caution, looks at the question of the desirability of these developments against a wider background. In particular it suggests that the use of AI technology offers a chance for legislators (those who make the law) to gain advantage over the judiciary (those who implement the law). This is a change in the constitutional balance of power that could have extremely unfortunate social consequences. These developments are made more worrying by the fact that those who will be most affected by them are largely unaware of them. What is obviously needed is a far wider debate about these sorts of possibilities. It is unfortunate that academic specialisations prevent more people discussing the social impact of AI in this area. It is an area where ideas exported from AI are already having tremendous social impact. No doubt this will be both good and bad in the long term, but it should not be allowed to proceed without serious discussion and analysis.

Applying AI and similar computing techniques to the legal area raises a number of new social, and political, problems. Not only are there no clear solutions to these problems, but it is not yet apparent which groups will assume responsibility for finding solutions. This situation will have to be changed. The next three chapters move from the legal area to begin an exploration of the relationship between AI and morality. Although this may seem an obscure area to some, it is the focal point of many of the issues raised by a consideration of the influence from new technologies. The discussions of the social implications of the use of AI in law suggest that there may be special problems about the use of AI to take certain decisions that have a particularly human element. There does not seem to be any consensus about to which particular decisions this applies. It is certainly not too soon to begin to establish what sort of limits apply to the use of non-human systems in the moral area.

Initiating a sober and realistic debate on the relationship between AI and morality is difficult because of the sort of attitudes that people bring to the discussion. One way of analysing these attitudes is to use the division into three groups mentioned above. It is clear that the Disbelievers will argue that there is nothing to be discussed in this area. They will contend that the very idea of AI systems making or assisting in moral judgements is absurd, only human beings can do this. The Believers, on the other hand, will feel that the social implications of this sort of work are generally positive. This would seem to leave only the Social Critics who might want to explore the problems raised by this area in any great detail.

However, there are matters of interest to all three groups. For example, Chapter 7,The Computer Representation of Moral Reasoning, examines some of the ways in which present-day AI technology might handle the special problems of performing moral reasoning. The crudity of present techniques will not convince the Disbelievers that AI can handle moral reasoning, but should serve to show that it can do something similar enough to moral reasoning to enable some AI enthusiasts to use it for this sort of purpose. The dangers of technological positivism should be remembered in this context.

Chapter 8, Implications of the Computer Representation of Moral Reasoning, is an attempt to deal with the issues that previous chapters have only touched upon. In particular it asks: 'is it right to do this sort of research?' and: 'what are the social implications of the widespread use of AI systems to perform or assist with moral and ethical judgements?'. These questions, particularly the former, are of great relevance to the Believers. This group need to participate in the debate over how to develop this technology to the benefit of all mankind, just as much as do the Disbelievers and Social Critics.

The overall conclusion of this chapter is that it is morally correct to perform this sort of research in spite of clear dangers. The alternative course of not developing this area would lead to AI becoming progressively more competent, but not necessarily incorporating the human values that we ought at least to try to include. It is worth reminding readers, particularly those with a philosophical background, that the purpose of this book is to initiate the widest possible discussion of issues to which there is a certain urgency. This is particularly true of this area, where technical possibilities are developing quickly.

Speculation on more remote possibilities is taken to the extreme in Chapter 9, The potential moral rights and duties of Intelligent Artifacts: robot morality is not a subject for science fiction. Just as in the legal sphere there is a need to discuss non-human agency, sooner or later we will have to confront the possibility that there might be some sort of artifacts which have moral duties and which some people may claim also have moral rights. The question which then has to be answered is 'what sort of moral rights and duties?' These may or may not be identical or similar to human moral rights and duties. The sort of problem with which we shall have to deal might be expressed as: 'what shall we put in the robot's conscience?'

I am aware that this sort of discussion will offend or even anger some people but it is necessary for the sort of reasons discussed in the previous sections. AI is already producing systems that manipulate knowledge and venturing into the manipulation of ethical knowledge. There are great dangers in ignoring the problems of robot morality. If we want AI systems to function for the benefit of humanity then it is essential that we at least attempt to put the appropriate values into them. Deciding what are appropriate values is problematic, but the time to initiate discussion is now!

Chapter 6, Ethical AI takes a different perspective on the relationship between AI and ethics. It emphasises the need for those involved with AI to pay attention to ethical matters, and in particular to behave in a more ethical manner than they have so far, thus it is a cautionary tale for the Believers. During the AI boom of the 1980s little attention was paid to ethics in AI research or the marketing of AI products. It is to be hoped that the subsequent reduction of commercial interest in AI may well prompt an improvement in this position. This chapter insists that ethics are not an expensive luxury, but an essential and profitable part of both commercial and academic AI. Because of this, it is claimed, there are reasons to hope that a more ethical attitude will prevail in the future.

The last chapter, The Virtual Sky is Not The Limit deals with the allegedly novel technology of Virtual Reality (VR). Like AI, VR appears to introduce a number of difficult moral questions. In spite of the apparent novelty of the technology, at least some of these questions can be shown to be variations on more familiar moral problems. Examining these issues is at least a start towards developing a basis for discussion of the social and moral implications of VR.

However, familiar or not, many of the moral problems raised by VR need urgent attention and discussion. Just as with AI, VR is a technology that can generate powerful ideas. The combination of AI and VR technologies is also highly probable. No doubt VR will also generate its Believers, Disbelievers and Social Critics. The remarks made in previous sections about AI apply, more or less, in equal measure to VR.

Notes

1. 'Positivism' is one of the most overworked words in philosophy and a full account would be outside the scope of the present discussion. However, a common feature of all types of positivism is the desire to provide a method of terminating debate at some point: particularly debate which seems open-ended or interminable. Various methods have been proposed over the centuries, primarily a view of science as (in principle) yielding certainty. The technological positivist is firmly rooted in this tradition, proposing various technological (usually AI-based) methods of avoiding open-ended philosophical or social debate.

References

Boden, M. (1981). 'Human Values in a Mechanistic Universe' in Boden, M. Minds and Mechanisms, Harvester, Brighton, pp.265-295.

Council for Science and Society (CSS) (1989). Benefits and Risks of Knowledge-Based Systems, OUP.

Feigenbaum, E.A. (1993). Tiger in a Cage, Distinguished Lecture Series VI, University Video Communications, Stanford.

McDermott, D.A. (1987). A Critique of Pure Reason Computational Intelligence 3, pp.151-160.

Turkle, S. (1984). The Second Self, Computers and the Human Spirit, pp.281-327.

Whitby, B.R. (1984). 'AI: some immediate dangers' in Artificial Intelligence: Human Effects Yazdani and Narayanan (eds) Ellis Horwood, Chichester, pp.235-236.

Whitby B.R. (1988). AI: A Handbook of Professionalism, Ellis Horwood, Chichester, pp.24-38.

The Social implications of AI

Does AI have Social Implications?

AI is a curious project – part technology, part philosophy, and part other methods of research into human, animal and other minds. It is this curious nature that makes it so difficult to assess its social implications. We have some idea of how to assess the social implications of technology, and perhaps even of scientific projects, but this combination is something new and difficult. Lack of clarity about just what AI is often lends a taint of unreality to discussions of its social implications.

This problem is often compounded by a reluctance of those directly involved with AI to consider the area of social implications. They may argue that it is 'none of our business' even though it clearly is. Or they may argue that AI can have social implications only when, and to the extent that, it delivers widely-used technologies. This excuse also fails to withstand close scrutiny: AI has had an influence out of all proportion to its ability to deliver useful technology and that influence has profound social consequences. This is an issue that will be developed further in this and subsequent chapters.

As a technology, AI has, so far, very few social implications: it remains a fairly esoteric area of research. Although AI has produced a surprisingly large number of useful working products, from time-sharing operating systems to expert systems, these are inevitably seen more as by-products than as true successes. Very often, a technological success in AI is appropriated by computer science or the relevant branch of engineering. One important reason for this is that AI rarely seems to forget completely the goal (whether it be declared or not) of producing an artefact that is more or less human-like in its intelligence. It is argued in Chapter 3 that this is not a proper goal for AI, considered either as a technology or as a science. However, excessive consideration of this goal leads to a focus on the social implications of the widespread use of artefacts (often expected to be robots or computers) that are intelligent in a very similar way to human beings. Since this is not in prospect, a more realistic analysis of the social implications of AI should really look at other areas.

Some of these will be considered in detail in subsequent chapters. In particular Chapters 4 and 5 consider some of the impacts of AI in the area of legal practice. This chapter considers the impacts of AI in the areas of employment and unemployment, safety-critical applications, and the centralisation of power. It is also necessary to spend some time discussing the question of whether or not AI has a dehumanising influence, and the dangers of both experts and commentators continuing to sensationalise and over-sell AI. These are among the real and immediate social implications of AI.

As has already been observed (Chapter 1), AI's main social impact stems from its abilities to generate ideas that have influence outside AI.These have caused other disciplines to change in ways that may in turn have more immediate social consequences. For a wide range of reasons people tend to look in the wrong sort of areas for the social implications of AI. Philosophical interest has generally tended to focus on questions of whether or not A.I. can achieve the objective of human-like intelligence, and if this, or any part of it, can be achieved, what this implies for our understanding of human intelligence. The latter question is obviously of interest to many branches of psychology. The narrowness of focus is not helped by the widespread citation of the so-called Turing test (discussed in detail in the next chapter) and by the widespread use of definitions of AI that take humans as a starting point. Perhaps the most popular of these is Minsky's: "Artificial intelligence is the science of making machines do things that would require intelligence if done by men" (Minsky 1968) Even if we ignore the obvious facts that AI is not interested in some intelligent activities (such as dancing) and that machines are often made to do things that require intelligence when done by humans (such as driving trains or building cars) by sciences other than AI, this definition is still unfortunate in its reference to human performance. In this respect it follows the tradition set up by the Turing test of referring to human intelligence as some sort of yardstick. This tends to confirm the focus on human-like intelligence in AI. If we look for the social implications of AI in the consequences of producing artificial human beings we will probably miss the real action.

The rather strange conclusion suggested by this analysis is that AI is likely to remain influential (as, in fact, it has been so far) in ways other than by widespread use of its products[1]. The influence of AI on the academic world in particular has been spectacular: psychologists and philosophers have found themselves compelled to respond (both positively and negatively) to AI. Since it is unlikely that it is some piece of spectacular AI technology that has required a response it must be the ideas thrown out by AI that need response. It is in this process that the most important sort of social implications of AI are generated.

A History of AI

The history of AI is one of successive periods of optimism and disappointments. This is often remarked upon, but less often observed in print are some of the causes of this unfortunate history. Most important among these is the repeated tendency to dismiss earlier approaches to AI as completely mistaken. It is this tendency which tends to give the impression of a series of failures when what has, in fact, occurred is a series of successes. It is also worth repeating that although many portray AI as an unsuccessful branch of computer science, the reverse is historically the case. In other words, computation is one of the many facets of human intelligent activity which have been sucessfully reproduced by AI. AI successes, of which computation is the most spectacular, tend to be seen as no longer the province of AI.

Any overview of the history of AI [2] should include the observation that from the mid 1950s to the mid 1960s the primary direction of A.I research was into algorithmic approaches to problem solving. Almost all this work would now be seen as part of the general theory of computation. The common technical approach behind almost all successful AI research during this period was the technique of reducing a problem of whatever sort to a 'search' operation. The main insight was that a great many different sorts of problem could be formalised into a starting position, a finishing position (or goal), and a set of moves that might or might not lead from one to the other. The main successes of this period were in the areas of game-playing (such as chess) programs and in theorem proving. This period of AI has left us with readily available chess-playing computers and a wide variety of successful small-scale products that have been assimilated into the computer industry in general.

These approaches were abandoned during the period between the late 1960s and the mid 1970s in favour of approaches which took far more account of human methods of problem solving. The main research efforts of this period were into the problems of getting computers to understand natural human languages, such as English, or to analyse human stories and dialogues. During this period there was much more input from psychology than had been the case in the previous period. Particularly important was the work of Quillian (1968) that introduced the notion of a structured representation of knowledge into the field of AI. A typical successful program of this period was Winograd's SHRDLU (Winograd 1972) that, at least seemed, to enabled a computer to learn and understand language, albeit within a highly circumscribed and artificial domain. Neither Winograd, nor any other important AI figure saw any point in continuing with this line of research, which is significant for present purposes.

An important reason for this was that a major new fashion had swept through AI around the mid 1970s: a rejection of the quest for general problem-solving methods in favour of using explicit detailed knowledge about how to solve a specific problem. This line of research also yielded significant successes. Knowledge-based systems, or expert systems as they came to be known, could give impressive performance (often better than human experts) within a suitable and narrow area of expertise. In the early part of this period there was a hangover from the previous period in that many researchers sought to deliberately imitate the methods of knowledge representation and reasoning used by human experts. However, towards the end of this period it was becoming apparent that human methods were often not optimal, particularly in areas such as reasoning with uncertain information, and that expert systems could do better.

The fact that expert systems were often useful and relatively easy to build led to an AI boom and forced AI into the world of industry. AI companies sprang up in various countries offering expert systems as solutions to a wide variety of real-world problems. However this boom was over almost as soon as it had begun. A major technical problem was and is that real-world, useful knowledge is expensive to obtain and time-consuming to build into an expert system's knowledge base. However, the fledgling AI industry really did not help itself at this time. Most AI researchers were uneasy with the idea of agreed standards for the interchange of knowledge bases between different expert systems and with the need to move the technology from the 'one-off' custom product into standardised products. The reluctance of AI to behave as an industry rather than an esoteric area of research at this time has been remarked upon (Feigenbaum 1993), but once again events were overtaken by a radically new approach to AI.

By the mid-to late-1980s, the cutting edge of AI research had moved into the area of neural nets or Parallel Distributed Processing (PDP). This line of research appeared to have very little in common with preceding AI work. PDP abandoned conventional approaches to computing in favour of approaches based upon inspiration from the organisation of human and animal brains. Almost all previous approaches to AI had accepted that digital computers were sufficiently flexible and powerful to support intelligence, at least in principle, and the task of AI was, in essence, simply to write software that was clever enough. Critics of this approach had been very much on the fringe of AI until the mid-to late-1980s when it became possible to formalise methods of programming (or training) for what were, in theory, very different sorts of computers, generically known as neuralets.

A conventional stored-program digital computer is strongly based upon the theoretical device known as a Turing machine. What this means in practice is that all of its operations, no matter how complex, are composed of isolated single steps (usually the moving of a number of electronic switches from on to off or vice-versa) performed in sequence. The sequence is typically under the constant control of a single device known as the central processing unit (CPU). The art of programming such a machine consists of combining millions of such simple steps into an interesting performance, such as word-processing or giving expert advice.

Neural nets by contrast have a completely different arrangement. A number of processing units operate in parallel, passing simple non-structured messages to each other across the entire network (hence the term Parallel Distributed Processing). Computation in a neural net takes the form of changing patterns of activation levels for the net as a whole, rather than the form of a sequence of single steps. Significantly, this approach to computation is not based upon the manipulation of explicit symbols, as had been most previous approaches, but is often called 'subsymbolic'. This is loosely based upon the way in which human and animal brains are thought to operate, performance being the result of activation patterns in a large number of brain cells or neurons. It is important not to stretch the analogy between natural brains and neural nets too far as there are many important differences and the similarity is of a fairly superficial kind.

However, from the mid-1980s to the mid-1990s, this new approach (like the others before it) yielded many interesting and exciting results. Neural nets proved adept at certain tasks that had been extremely difficult for previous AI approaches. For example there were successes at tasks that involved recognising incomplete or distorted examples of a typical pattern, as we do when we recognise handwriting or the sounds in speech. Their performance also had interesting superficial similarities to human brains. Memory took place as a pattern distributed over the entire network, rather than at a single location; there were superficial similarities in learning, and they responded to damage by a gradual general deterioration in performance, rather than the brittle failure pattern of previous systems.

Neural net research has not yet been abandoned in the way that previous approaches to AI seem to have been. This, however, may not be far away because, as with previous approaches, the initial enthusiasm has been replaced by realising the size of the problems and fewer claims that many of the large and difficult problems of AI will be solved very quickly. To this must be added the fact that PDP has already lost its status as the trendiest place to be.

The latest trend is variously called 'situated robotics', or 'artificial life' and is characterised (once again) by wholesale rejection of most of the theoretical burden of all previous approaches to A.I. in favour of an approach that is much more rooted in biology. Generalisations about such a new area are unwise because approaches differ. Some researchers follow nature as a design method using 'genetic algorithms' or a computational analogue of evolution by natural selection to actually 'evolve' the control systems of their robots (Cliff, Harvey, Husbands 1993) while others adopt a more hands-on approach to trying to copy nature (Brooks 1992). Nonetheless, certain common features of this approach can be detected. In particular, great importance is placed on intelligence as situated, true of a particular organism (or robot) in a particular environment, but not true of the organism (or robot) when considered as separate from its environment. This approach is also holistic in a way that the previous approaches to AI have not been, in the sense that it rejects the possibility of separating (even in theory) the *vision* problem for an intelligent entity from the *planning* problem, or any of the other divisions that AI had previously tended to use.

Presenting these approaches in chronologically has the unfortunate consequence of suggesting that one replaced another because of some intrinsic superiority. This is an entirely false suggestion. If one has no partisan axe to grind then it must be said that they have all yielded useful and interesting results, which is something that is rarely acknowledged by the public at large. Indeed, all these approaches are continuing at various levels to yield interesting and useful results, and this is something rarely acknowledged even with in AI. Many successful products of AI research are simply integrated into other technologies; typically, but not exclusively, computer science and consumer electronics.

The reason for AI failing to get as much credit as it deserves is mainly the way in which these approaches have tended to supersede each other. The proponents of each new approach, while understandably enthusiastic about that approach, have expended too much energy condemning previous approaches. Not only does this mean that there is a lack of public (and even AI specialist) awareness of the achievements of previous approaches, but also that attempts to combine different approaches are lamentably few. AI practitioners reading this will, no doubt, want to shout 'Funding!' at this stage. It is true that funding for combining previous AI approaches with existing ones is generally harder to obtain than funding for an entirely new project. However, this is mainly because each new approach to A.I. has taken the short-sighted approach of making itself look attractive to funding bodies by contrasting itself sharply with previous failed attempts. This game has led to the widespread myth that AI's history of interesting partial successes is a history of failures.

To this must be added the great A.I. failing of 'hype'. This is perhaps the social implication of AI with which everyone connected to the field could and should be most concerned. Just as successive approaches to A.I. have found it necessary to describe previous approaches as failures, they have vastly increased the chances of their own approach being subsequently labelled a failure by making exaggerated promises and predictions. This is one of the reasons why the concentration on 'human-like performance' discussed in the previous section is still with us.

The exaggeration of AI's capabilities and rate of progress is reprehensible both as an unethical activity (a point taken up at length in Chapter 6) and as a negative influence on AI research. To pick a contemporary example, it is very easy to get the attention of the press if one makes the claim that robots will be more intelligent than human beings in, say, 50 years [3]. It is also highly disingenuous. First every one of the approaches to AI described above has tried to extrapolate from its successes, however small, to the achievement of something rivalling or even surpassing human intelligence, which, of course, has turned out to be extremely naive.

More serious than this naivety is the fact that this hype causes unachievable expectations in both the public and funding bodies. With the inevitable failure to meet such excessive expectations comes disillusionment with the whole field of AI. In many more practical areas people who make claims that cannot be met and thereby spoil the field for responsible and irresponsible alike would be forced out of the area by the relevant professional body. Perhaps this should happen with AI.

Employment and Unemployment

A general economic principle has been established that new technologies usually only cause unemployment during a transitional period. Following this, higher levels of economic activity and employment are generated by their widespread application. This is not to deny or detract from the very real disruption and deprivation that may well be incurred during the transitional phase.

The higher levels of economic activity and employment following the transitional phase are not usually a return to the patterns that existed before the technology was introduced. The jobs and markets are likely to be very different from those existing previously. In classical economic terms, technological innovations prevent economic stagnation as the extra profits due to innovation provide the essential stimulus for economic growth. This is sometimes seen as the reason for cyclical fluctuations in economic activity (Schumpeter 1934) and sometimes as a steady process determined by other aspects of economic activity (Kaldor and Mirrlees 1961).

Although there is not complete agreement on the economic processes involved, almost all economists would stress the need for the labour market to be flexible in response to technological innovation, mainly for the reasons outlined in the last paragraph. If a technological change, such as the widespread introduction of AI, brings about the removal of certain types of jobs and the creation of others, the best response is clearly to change the workers to meet the changed market.

How does this economic theory apply in the case of AI? Let us consider first, the case of Information Technology (IT) in general. Although many people will have lost their jobs as a result of the introduction of IT, it can be safely described as in general capital-replacing, rather than labour-replacing. For example, more accurate stock control is one of the benefits that IT can offer. An efficient computer system will usually allow a manufacturer to keep much smaller inventories, which may well be accompanied by an increase in employment levels, particularly in the data-processing (DP) department. Indeed, one of the most important changes in modern business practice has been the reduction in the holding of stocks at all points of the manufacturing and distribution process.

IT can also offer improved communication facilities, and although these are not so obviously capital-replacing as improved stock control, they have not been labour-replacing. Global communications are an important asset for modern industrial and commercial practice, but there is no obvious group of workers who are made unemployed by them. It is highly probable that the improvement in communications made possible by IT has resulted in a net increase in employment.

On balance, it would seem that IT is no different from previous technological innovations. It may bring about changes in the nature of work and a certain amount of temporary upheaval, but there is no good reason to see it as generating permanent unemployment. This is not to deny that some workers have lost jobs, and will continue to lose them as a result of the introduction of IT; this is obviously true of some clerical occupations, such as filing and stock-control clerks. Rather it is to assert that there is no reason not to expect the familiar pattern of the eventual generation of a greater total of jobs, albeit in rather different areas.

Some readers may wonder why these very general theoretical claims are not backed up by empirical research. There is no shortage of such research, but little to be gained in considering it here, for a number of reasons. First employment trend figures, if collected over a wide area, become unreliable. For example, if one wishes to look at trends in the number of jobs generated within the IT industry, should one collate the total of all employees of IT-related businesses, including cleaners, security guards, receptionists and the like? If this policy is adopted then the trend of the total may reflect more the total number and size of IT businesses than employment trends. Self-employed IT consultants will employ very few such support staff and long-established businesses moving into the IT area will already have sufficient support staff and will not make much impression on the trend statistics as a result. On the other hand, small and medium-sized firms will tend to recruit proportionately more support staff.

Attempting to measure the proportion of people who work directly with IT poses just as many problems. Since the IT industry is not highly professionalised, there is no ready demarcation between those who work directly with IT and those whose work is essentially unchanged, but whose workplace now contains computers (e.g. the secretarial professions).

Some researchers have adopted the more useful approach of examining the relative proportions of workers working in IT-related areas within established businesses. This gives a statistical measure of the rise of the DP department, but it does not show whether or not IT is creating or destroying jobs. Some businesses are more suitable for computerisation than others, and what this approach tends to measure is the change in employment activities in those concerns that are both successful and introducing IT. These two trends may or may not be related.

Even if we apply the simplifying assumptions that the rise of the DP department is always a cause of a rise in profitability, and that the businesses concerned would have failed if they had not increased the proportion of staff in their DP departments, there is still no obvious correlation between this proportion of employees and the overall employment trend. It would be possible, at one extreme, to argue that all jobs in IT-using businesses are IT-created jobs if the concern would have failed without IT, but this obvious absurdity must be balanced against the even greater one of looking at all redundancies and business failures as consequences of the failure to introduce appropriate IT.

More important than the practical difficulties in finding reliable measures is the fact that the labour market has been, and will continue to be, affected by other forces that seem more important than IT in determining the overall level of employment. The first of these is the existence of various fluctuating cycles of economic activity that, although centuries old, seem likely to continue generating periods of alternate high and low demand for labour. The second is the ending of the so-called cold war, the economic effects of which seem to have been both poorly forecast and also considerably greater than the introduction of IT. All of this makes any attempt to obtain accurate measures of the number of jobs which have been created or destroyed by IT very difficult.

So far, we have seen good reasons to reject simplistic assertions like: 'computers put people out of work', or its negative. There remain many important questions about the different types and textures of work that will result from the introduction of IT. It remains only to consider the differences, if any, between IT in general and AI with respect to their employment impact.

The Employment Effects of AI

Most of the preceding economic arguments about IT in general also apply in the special case of AI. To the extent that AI is considered as a technological development, then it will be subject to the same transitional phase. Of course, it has already been observed that there are other ways to look at AI than as a technological development. However, for the purpose of considering employment effects, it is reasonable to suspend these considerations and look at AI as a special case of IT.

There are, however, important differences in emphasis. AI is ostensibly much more concerned with labour replacement. If a great deal of research is put into enabling an artefact to perform a task previously undertaken by humans, it is safe to assume that (if the research turns out to be successful) similar artefacts will probably be employed in place of human workers to perform that task. Of course, a major economic motivation for doing this will be to justify the research expenditure. It is for this reason that the 'pure science' tag hangs rather uneasily on AI from the public's point of view. If you are worried about losing your job then it would seem rational to be equally worried about research which attempts to produce some sort of machine that can perform your job.

This does not mean that AI research cannot be seen as pure science or that all AI research should be opposed as potentially creating unemployment. It is a fact, though one not apparent to general public, that an extremely small proportion of AI research is concerned with the production of artefacts that could ever replace humans in employment. The expert system boom of the late 1980s, discussed above, appeared to threaten the employment of all various professionals, yet this threat has not materialised. The reasons for the non-materialisation of this threat are complex. First, as stated previously, the capabilities of the so-called expert systems were exaggerated while in reality they were in not comparable to the capabilities of human experts. Second, since expert systems generally deliver advice as output, a natural use for them is as advisory systems for professionals. This is taken up in various ways in subsequent chapters. For present purposes, it is sufficient to note that in comparison to the much larger economic factors mentioned in the preceding section, the employment effect of AI has been very small indeed historically.

The view that the employment effects of AI are likely to remain small has been challenged, most notably by Nilsson (Nilsson 1984). He accepts the general economic arguments of the last section, but maintains that AI is different from previous technologies in at least two important ways. First, he claims AI is likely to exceed human capabilities within the foreseeable future. Therefore, to the extent that AI will, like previous technologies generate new jobs, these will be jobs that can also be performed by AI. Second, AI is very cheap, at least when the marginal cost of running an AI system is considered. That is to say, with a certain level of computing facilities, running AI programs on them adds little or nothing to operating costs. Given these two assumptions, he predicts widespread displacement of human labour by AI. In addition Nilsson is not advocating any Luddite resistance to these changes; rather he is making a call to action by governments to make widespread economic and social reforms in anticipation of these changes.

If one grants his two assumptions about the differences between A.I. and previous technological innovations, then Nilsson's argument seems overwhelming. All that might be said against it is that the new jobs generated might tend to be in areas that were primarily about human contact and thus not automatically threatened by AI. Nilsson tends to assume that the major area of human employment is in the production of material goods. This is the area of employment that is most threatened by automation of all sorts, including AI. The assumption that employment is primarily for the production of material goods might well be challenged. There seems to be no obvious limit to employment possibilities in areas that are mainly about human-to-human contact, and therefore not threatened by automation.

However, there are reasons to question both of Nilsson's assumptions. On the likelihood of AI exceeding human capabilities in a general sense, it must be repeated that this does not appear technically possible for the foreseeable future. This does not mean that there will be no displacement of human labour, but that the displacement process may be much slower than Nilsson envisages. However, even if the process were to accelerate there would be serious questions about whether it was desirable except in certain isolated fields. Much of this book is an attempt to focus attention on these questions. On the second assumption, while granting that the marginal cost of running an AI system is very low, the same cannot be said of designing and building AI systems. The cost of AI research is very high in proportion to the commercial value of the useful systems produced. This has worked historically to maintain the very low employment impact of AI, and will probably continue to do so in the future.

Much depends on the answers to the questions as to the nature and goals of AI raised at the beginning of the chapter. However it behoves those working in AI to be very sensitive to this issue. They could certainly do much more to reassure the public that AI has very little prospect of causing mass unemployment. Better, clearer, and less use of hyperbole in presentations of AI would certainly help to reassure the public that AI is not aimed at putting people out of work.

Despite the observations in the preceding section about the difficulty of measuring the changes in employment caused by a particular technology, it is reasonable to assert that AI has rendered very few people unemployed. Some expert systems may have displaced human expertise in medical, legal, and engineering applications, but this effect has been truly minimal. Similarly, automation in various parts of manufacturing has undoubtedly displaced human labour (though it is very difficult, if not impossible, to say how much), and AI may have made a small contribution to this automation. Again, it is safe to say that this is minimal.

Indeed, AI has had surprisingly little direct impact on the industrial and commercial world considering its impact on the academic sphere. Its employment impacts certainly come nowhere near the fanciful predictions of some enthusiasts. It might well be argued that the main reason for this is the failure of the research to produce working technology. A more accurate description would be that although AI has produced many technical successes, it has repeatedly failed to live up to the more extravagant promises made.

It is *just* possible that as yet unforeseen technical breakthroughs might change all this. Perhaps intelligent assistants or domestic robots may become widespread. It is even possible that intelligent computers will somehow emerge and pass the Turing test. While chapter 3 explains why this is not a practical or worthwhile goal for AI, It is also the case that the necessary technical advances are not in prospect. In considering the employment effects of AI it is therefore sensible to disregard these possibilities.

As was remarked in the last chapter, people tend to think of past historical trends in order to understand the likely impact of new technologies such as AI. A major effect of the industrial revolution was disruption in employment. It is natural to look for similar massive disruption in the case of IT and perhaps even in the case of AI. There seems to be no evidence of such disruption, with employment levels still affected more by the overall level of economic activity in a given country than by new technology.

Of course, the lack of impact of AI on overall employment levels does not imply any lack of impact with respect to the 'texture' of work. The tasks actually performed at work may be substantially altered by AI. While it is difficult to generalise, we might expect that the ability of new technology to search through, manipulate and even recognise patterns in large amounts of information to reduce the need for humans to perform that sort of task. The ability of AI systems to diagnose and give advice in highly-specialised areas may reduce the ability of humans to demand large salaries for doing so. The technical problems involved in building common-sense and general knowledge into AI systems may well mean that human expertise in these areas is more highly regarded and highly rewarded.

It should also finally be observed that many people are still employed primarily to perform tasks that are boring, hazardous, or in other ways extremely unpleasant. Provided (and this is by no means an empty proviso) that these people can be adequately rewarded for doing something else during working hours, it is morally right to attempt to develop artefacts that will perform those tasks instead. The moral imperative involved is that of developing technology so as to reduce human suffering and this should always take precedence over purely economic considerations.

Safety-Critical AI

Much attention has recently been given to the problems of incorporating software into so-called safety-critical applications. These are growing in number and significance, and include such things as vehicle and aircraft control systems, automatic control of nuclear and chemical plants, automated weapons systems, and so on. One very important reason for concern is that any problem with computer software in such applications has potentially disastrous consequences.

The software industry has a record of producing products that contain bugs, testing its products by selling them to customers, and often (rather surprisingly often) marketing a product that does not work at all. Compared to other industries, the culture of the software industry is still lamentably slapdash and amateurish. This has led some commentators (for example Smith 1985, and Partridge 1986) to suggest that error-free software is an impossible dream.

What difference does AI make to this? Firstly, it is highly unlikely that AI will lead to more reliable software. In general, AI products are harder to control and predict than are conventional computer products, though it must be stressed that this is not always the case. Attention has been drawn to some of the problems with producing safe and reliable AI software. These accounts, however, concentrate on AI techniques such as search-based problem solvers and knowledge-based systems. There are many difficulties in the production of AI products suitable for use in safety-critical applications (see Partridge 1986, Whitby 1988). These problems do not completely rule out the use of AI in safety-critical applications, however they make AI an unattractive option, compared with more conventional computing techniques. These works only really consider approaches to AI which have become known as GOFAI (Good Old-Fashioned AI): they do not consider the safety implications of AI approaches based on neural nets, genetic algorithms, or situated robotics. However, the problems GOFAI has in producing software for safety-critical applications are as nothing compared to the problems which must be faced by the newer approaches to AI (these have been called collectively nouvelle AI). Software that uses some sort of neural net or genetic algorithm must face the further problem that it seems, often almost by definition, to be 'inscrutable'. By this, I mean that the exact rules that would enable us to completely predict its operation are not and often never can be available. We can know that it works and test it over a number of cases but we will not in the typical case ever be able to know exactly how. The reason for this inscrutability is simple. If we knew exactly how then we could employ an algorithmic or rule-based solution. These are almost always quicker, cheaper and more reliable than more sophisticated AI techniques.

At present, many of the most attractive applications for nouvelle AI are in areas such as low-level vision and pattern recognition, where their inscrutability does not really matter. However, advocates of these newer AI approaches have to face this problem as soon as their technology leaves the laboratory and enters real world applications. This means that the problem cannot be postponed, since both neural nets and genetic algorithms are finding many real world applications.

It seems that there are a number of approaches that we might take to the problem of inscrutable AI in safety-critical applications. The most obvious, and in many ways the worst approach would be to argue from a weak analogy with human beings. That is to say that human beings are in some sense evolved and have some brain features superficially similar to neural nets and therefore that AI products incorporating these features are at least as safe as a human operator would be. This is the worst approach to this problem for two main reasons.

First, even if it were true that the risks involved with such inscrutable AI technology were only of the same order of those involved with the use of human operators, this would not be good enough for most safety-critical applications. Human beings are extremely error-prone and we generally expect a significant improvement in this area from any automated system. In addition, we know a great deal about how to train, punish, reward, stress, relax, test, and monitor human operators. Any novel technology presenting a similar level of risk would inevitably suffer until knowledge comparable to that we have about humans could be built up. In all probability, this would would take decades (though, given the fact that these are artefacts, not humans, we would could hope for slightly greater insight into the internal mechanisms than is the case with humans).

Second, the weak analogy with human beings is in reality very weak indeed. The fact that a human is an evolved creature and that a piece of software has undergone a process loosely analogous to biological evolution will very rarely, if ever, permit comparisons of their respective performance in safety-critical situations. The analogies between human brain structure and Neural Nets are similarly more to do with inspiration than copying. Although certain types of Neural Net can be arranged sometimes to display superficially human-like performance, so can most other types of software (ELIZA for example). The analogy is too weak to deal with the legitimate worries about safety-critical applications of these sorts of software.

If we abandon the weak analogy with humans, there are some better approaches to this problem that are worthy of consideration. The first would be to adopt an attitude to testing *in situ* that placed more stress on this than is the case with conventional AI. If software is 'inscrutable' then it would seem that it should be tested far more extensively and expected to behave less predictably than software that is understood more fully. Of course, in many, if not most, cases the testing could not be exhaustive and the simple slogan 'Test more' is unlikely to reassure either the public or the experts in this area, especially in view of the remarks already made about the software industry having a lamentable track record. What is important is to foster an improvement in the attitude to testing that ceases to tolerate the sale of incomplete and bug-ridden products. An even better idea still would be to combine the new approaches to AI with monitoring programs using conventional algorithmic techniques designed to prevent most forseeable mishaps. This would not usually create technical difficulties and could even be made an engineering requirement for neural net and genetic algorithm-based products in safety-critical areas. An enforced 'health warning' could similarly be required spelling out the inscrutable, and in some cases unpredictable, nature of these approaches to AI.

This is a large area where the bulk of the work has yet to be undertaken. The flavour of AI research tends to be more about exploring possibilities and simply getting the technology to work than about considering safety implications. There are many text books to be written on the subject of safety-critical AI. A practitioner once suggested that a few 'minor' accidents would be desirable to focus the minds of governments and professional organisations on the task of producing safe AI (Bobrow and Hayes 1985). Perhaps we could start before then.

Is AI Dehumanizing?

Some writers have claimed that the development of AI will encourage a view of human beings as more mechanistic, for example, Rogers(1984) claims that AI is a fundamental challenge to humanism. The case against this has been argued passionately by Boden (particularly in Boden 1981). Before attempting to analyse the respective viewpoints it is worth stressing that this debate is not about AI technology but is once again about A.I-generated ideas.

The basis of Rogers' claim is that despite the AI proponents protestations that their concepts of a machine are sufficiently complex to allow for sufficient depth of features to avoid any devaluation of human psychology, AI is firmly rooted in a tradition of a mechanistic view of mind. This proposes that possibility of reproducing all, or even some important part, of human intelligence in a machine suggests that human intelligence is mechanistic and the claim detracts from human values such as freedom and dignity. Of course, the extreme position of this view would be that any attempt to either account for, or model, human intelligence detracts from human values. This would only leave us with views of human intelligence that see it as essentially mysterious.

Nonetheless, we need to take Rogers' criticisms seriously. To put such an extreme gloss on the criticism that AI is dehumanising, is an inadequate response to what is, quite possibly, a widespread public anxiety about AI that is not paralleled by public anxiety about scientific psychology. Of course, public anxiety is not always well founded. The general public have a view of the nature of machines which is very much at odds with the view set forward by those involved with AI such as Boden. The very vivid discrepancy between the public conception of a machine and the conception often used by those in AI is highlighted in a story from Turkle (Turkle 1984). She tells of spending a morning with a patient troubled by the fear that he is 'just a machine' by which he means that he has no control over, or emotional investment in, his life. In the afternoon she spends time with enthusiastic AI researchers who talk of how liberating it can be to 'see oneself as a machine'. By seeing oneself as a machine they mean something very different from the troubled patient. They have a view of a machine that includes the possibility of choice between different goals, making plans to achieve those goals, and even experiencing pleasure on attaining them.

The public view of a machine often tends, as was remarked in the last chapter, to be based more upon a ninteenth century kind of machine than the sorts that are considered within AI [4]. The situation is not helped by the hype discussed in this chapter and the influence of the Turing test discussed in the next chapter. Unfortunately, the public tend to be subjected to a picture of AI that is both inaccurate and disturbing. The Turing test suggests that AI has more or less complete replication of human intelligence as its long-term goal and the exaggerated claims made about various AI techniques suggests to the public that AI proposes to do this in a technically uninspired manner - it is this combination which appears dehumanizing.

Of course, this public conception is not accurate and AI should not be seen as committed either to replication of human intelligence or to a single technique. Boden has repeatedly stated the case for a more informed public conception (Boden 1977, 1981, 1990). There is no need to repeat Boden's claims here, suffice it so say that her view of what a machine might be certainly includes the possibility of a machine setting its own goals and in that sense at least being free. If the public's conception were more realistic about both the goals of AI and its achievements then the spectre of dehumanisation would, in all probability. disappear. Our knowledge of aerodynamics and even our ability to build flying artifacts has not reduced the wonder of natural flight or 'de-birdified' birds (Unless, that is, one maintains that all scientific explanations remove our sense of wonder at the natural world.)

This debate is really about the cultural traditions of Western science, philosophy, and psychology, rather than about AI itself. However, if, as has been urged in this and the preceding chapter, we move away from a picture of AI as irretrievably involved with the copying of human psychological features, it is possible that both sides are more likely to be reconciled.

Another way of responding to this debate would be to observe that AI can be dehumanising only if, and only to the extent, that we allow it to be. That is to say that there is a role for advocates of human values to stress their importance against those who are in awe of the technology (or perhaps in awe of some of the highly optimistic and exaggerated claims that are often made about the technology).

The Distribution of Benefits

One of the most important social implications of any technology is the way in which the benefits (and disbenefits) are distributed. It is essential to ask who the gainers and the losers from this technology will be.

In spite of the importance of this question it is often neglected, particularly by those actually developing the technology. Some may feel that it is none of their concern; some may argue that the first priority is to get the technology actually working and that questions about who gets the benefits can be postponed. Both these attitudes are unrealistic. First, the general public will tend to be more interested in the question of the distribution of benefits (and this can be taken to include employment effects) than in any other aspect of the technology. Second, since the development of nuclear weapons it has been obviously disingenuous for scientists to claim that they are merely exploring what is possible and that the use that society makes of their discoveries is none of their business, or that it can wait until they have got the technology to work.

In the case of AI there are many difficult, but interesting, questions about the distribution of benefits: many of these are considered in other chapters of this book. In particular, the effects of AI on legal practice and on the balance of power in the constitution are considered in Chapter 5. In general, the track record of AI is that, like much of IT, it has tended to be of more use to those who hold power and to concentrate more power in their hands. That is to say that many AI products and techniques tend to make control of operations (military, commercial, medical, informational) more reliable. This is of benefit, in many cases, to those who need control, and not for those who are likely to be controlled. There are exceptions: the use of AI techniques to make information more generally available and to improve education and training, for example, will usually tend to reduce the controllability of those who benefit from these applications of AI.

It is worth remarking upon the fact that a significant proportion of AI research has been directly or indirectly supported by military funding bodies, both in Britain and the U.S. This clearly indicates some parts of society that see themselves as potential gainers from AI. Can they be wrong?

Notes

1. At present the public image of AI is so poor that many companies resist using the label: 'AI' or variations on it for marketing reasons.

2. All histories are tendentious and this is no exception. Parts of it are due to Jackson (1986), but the contentious elements and the overall tone cannot be attributed elsewhere.

3. This claim is reported as being made by Kevin Warwick in 1995! In various places see for example Computing Sept 14th 1995.

4. The public (and some scientists') conception of a computer is similarly mistaken. Consider the widespread myths that 'computers can only do what they are told to do' and 'computers can only perform logical reasoning'. Both these myths are false, but their falsehood is of little consequence for most practical purposes - it is only in questions like whether or AI is dehumanizing that such mistakes matter.

References

Bobrow, D.G and Hayes, P.J. (eds)(1985), Artificial Intelligence - where are we? Artificial Intelligence 25. pp. 413-415.

Boden, M.A.(1977) Artificial Intelligence and Natural Man, Brighton, Harvester. pp.393-473.

Boden, M.A.(1981) Human Values in a Mechanistic University in Minds and Mechanisms, Brighton, Harvester. pp.265-295.

Boden, M.A.(1990) The Creative Mind, Myths and Mechanisms, London, Weidenfield and Nicholson. pp.263-266.

Brooks, R. (1992), Artificial Intelligence and Real Robots in Varela, F.J. and Bourgine, P. (eds) Towards a Practice of Autonomous Systems, Proceedings of the First European Conference on Artificial Life, Boston, Ma., MIT Press.

Cliff, D., Harvey, I., and Husbands, P. (1993) Explorations in evolutionary robotics. Adaptive Behaviour 2. pp.73-110.

Feigenbaum, E.A. (1993) Tiger in a Cage , Distinguished Lecture Series VI, Stanford, University Video Communications.

Jackson, P. (1968), Introduction to Expert Systems, Wokingham, Addison Wesley. pp. 2-11.

Kaldor, N. and Mirrlees, J.A.(1961-2) Growth Model with Induced Technical Progress in Sen, A. (ed),(1970) Growth Economics, Harmondsworth, Penguin. pp. 343-366.

Minsky, M.L. (1968) Semantic Information Processing, Boston, Ma., MIT Press, p.v.

Nilsson, N.J. (1984) Artificial Intelligence, Employment, and Income in Trappl (ed), (1985), Impacts of Artificial Intelligence, Amsterdam, North Holland.

Partridge, D. (1986) Artificial intelligence: applications in the future of software engineering, Chichester, Ellis Horwood.

Quillan, M. R. (1968) Semantic Memory in Minsky, M. (ed) (1968) Semantic Information Processing, Cambridge Mass, MIT Press. pp.227–70.

Rogers, I (1984) AI as a dehumanizing force in Yazdani and Narayanan (eds) AI Human Effects, Chichester, Ellis Horwood. pp.222-233.

Schumpeter, J.(1934) The Theory of Economic Development, Harvard University Press.

Smith, B.L. (1985), The Limits of Correctness, Presented at the Symposium on Uninentional Nuclear War, 5th Congress of the International Physicians for the Prevention of Nuclear War, Budapest June 1985.

Turing, A.M. (1950), Computing Machinery and Intelligence, Mind LIX 236(see Chapter 3 for a more detailed discussion of this paper and its consequences).

Turkle, S. (1984), The Second Self: Computers and the Human Spirit, Granada, pp. 328-329.

Whitby, B. (1988) AI A Handbook of Professionalism, Chichester, Ellis Horwood, pp. 74-83.

Winnograd, T. (1972), Understanding Natural Language, New York, Academic Press.

Why The Turing Test is AI's biggest blind alley

Alan Turing's 1950 paper, Computing Machinery and Intelligence (Turing 1950) and the Turing test suggested in it are rightly seen as inspirational to the inception and development of AI. However, inspiration can soon become distraction in science, and it is not too early to begin to consider whether or not the Turing test is just such a distraction. What this chapter argues is that this is indeed the case with the Turing test and AI.

AI has had an intimate relationship with the Turing test throughout its brief history. The view of this relationship, presented in this chapter, is that it has developed more or less as follows:

- **1950 - 1966**: A source of inspiration to all concerned with AI
- **1966 - 1973**: A distraction from some more promising avenues of AI research
- **1973 - 1990**: By now a source of distraction mainly to philosophers, rather than AI workers
- **1990**: Consigned to history. [1]

One conclusion that is implied by this view of the history of AI and Turing's 1950 paper is that for most of the period since its publication it has been a distraction. While not detracting from the brilliance of the paper and its central role in the philosophy of AI, it can be argued that Turing's 1950 paper, or perhaps some strong interpretations of it, has, on occasion, hindered both the practical development of AI and the philosophical work necessary to facilitate that development.

Thus one can make the claim that, in an important philosophical sense, Computing Machinery and Intelligence has led AI into a blind alley from which it only just beginning to extract itself. It is also an implication of the title of this chapter that the Turing test is not the only blind alley in the progress of AI. Although this chapter makes no examination of this implication, it is one that I am happy to accept.

One main source of this distraction has been the common, yet mistaken reading of Computing Machinery and Intelligence as somehow showing that one can attempt to build an intelligent machine without a prior understanding of the nature of intelligence. If we can, by whatever means, build a computer-based system that deceives a human interrogator for a while into suspecting that it might be human, then we have solved the many philosophical, scientific, and engineering problems of AI! This simplistic reading has, of course, proved both false and misleading in practice. The key to this would seem to be the mistaken view that Turing's paper contains an adequate operational definition of intelligence. A later section of this chapter suggests an interpretation of Computing Machinery and Intelligence and the 'imitation game' in their historical context. This interpretation does not imply the existence of an operational definition of intelligence.

That the paper was almost immediately read as providing an operational definition of intelligence is witnessed by the change from the label, 'imitation game' to 'Turing test' by commentators. Turing himself was always careful to refer to 'the game'. The suggestion that it might be some sort of test involves an important extension of Turing's claims. This is not some small semantic quibble, but an important suggestion that Turing's paper was being interpreted as closer to an operational test than he himself intended. If the Turing test is read as something like an operational definition of intelligence, then two very important defects of such a test must be considered. First, it is all or nothing: it gives no indication as to what a partial success might look like. Second, it gives no direct indications as to how success might be achieved. These two defects in turn have two weak implications. The first is that partial success is impossible, i.e. intelligence in computing machinery is an all-or-nothing phenomenon. The second is that the best route to this is by imitating human beings. Readers will see the flaws in these arguments without difficulty, no doubt, but it is hard to deny that much AI work has been distracted by a view of intelligence as a holistic phenomenon, demonstrated only by human beings, and only to be studied by the direct imitation of human beings.

To avoid the charge of setting up 'straw men', it will be argued in the remainder of this chapter that the general misreadings of Turing's 1950 paper have led to the currency of three specific mistaken assertions, namely:

1) Intelligence in computing machinery is (or is nearly, or includes) being able to deceive a human interlocutor.
2) The best approach to the problem of defining intelligence is through some sort of operational test, of which the 'imitation game' is a paradigm example.
3) Work specifically directed at producing a machine that could perform well in the 'imitation game' is genuine (or perhaps even useful) AI research.

This chapter will not pursue the falsity of Assertions 1 and 2 in any great detail. On Assertion 1 it should be sufficient to remark that the comparative success of ELIZA (Weizenbaum 1966), and programs like it, at deceiving human interlocutors could not be held to to indicate that they are closer to achieving intelligence than more sophisticated AI work. What we should conclude currently about this sort of AI work is that it represents research into the mechanisms of producing certain sorts of illusion in human beings rather than anything to do with intelligence, artificial or otherwise.

Other writers have convincingly attacked Assertion 2 on the grounds that the 'imitation game' does not test for intelligence but rather for other items such as cultural similarity (French 1996 and Michie 1996). Furthermore an all-or-nothing operational definition, such as that provided by the Turing test, is worse than useless for guiding research that is still at an early stage.

Assertion 3 and its effects on the history of AI are clearly the most important for the purposes of this book. A claim already made repeatedly in the previous two chapters is that work directed at success in the Turing test is neither genuine nor useful AI research. In particular, the point will be stressed that, irrespective of whether or not Turing's 1950 paper provided one, the last thing that AI has needed since 1966 is an operational definition of intelligence.

Few, if any, philosophers and AI researchers would assent to Assertion 3 being stated boldly. However, the influence of Alan Turing and his 1950 paper on the history of AI has been so profound that such mistaken claims can have a significant influence at a subconscious or subcultural level.

In any case, the passing of forty years gives sufficient historical perspective to enable us to begin to debate the way in which Computing Machinery and Intelligence has influenced the development of AI. The basic theme of this chapter is that the influence of Turing's 1950 paper has been largely unfortunate. This is not through any fault of the paper, but is rather a consequence of the historical circumstances that existed at the time of its writing and some of the pressures that have affected the subsequent development of AI.

Some Consequences of Misinterpretation of Computing Machinery and Intelligence

The main consequence of perceiving intelligence in terms of some sort of imitation of human performance, such as success in the imitation game, is that AI research and experiment has paid far too much attention to the development of machinery and programs that seek directly or indirectly to imitate human performance. It might, at first, be thought that this was inevitable since human behaviour is the only practical clue to the nature of intelligence that is readily available. However, this is a mistaken view. We know so very little about the nature of human intelligence that we cannot produce a definition that is of use to an AI engineer. Such a definition would have to make no direct reference to either humans or machines.

This focus of AI research on imitation of human performance has at least three unfortunate consequences. First it does not seem to have been very productive. Second, as I have argued at length elesewhere (Whitby 1988) it is unlikely to lead to profitable or safe applications of AI. New technology is generally taken up quickly where there is a clear deficiency in existing technologies and very slowly, if at all, where it offers only a marginal improvement over existing technologies. Even an amateur salesman of AI should be able to see that researchers should be steered away from programs that imitate human beings. The old quip about there being no shortage of natural intelligence contains an important truth. There are many safe, profitable applications for AI, but programs inspired by the imitation game are unlikely to lead towards them. This sort of research is more likely to produce interesting curiosities such as ELIZA than working AI applications.

A third unfortunate consequence is the way in which the myth that intelligence can be operationally defined as some sort of imitation of human beings has apparently exempted both philosophers and AI researchers from the rather difficult task of providing the sort of definition of intelligence that would be of use to AI. To be useful in AI research any definition of intelligence needs to be independent of human capabilities for a number of reasons. Among these are the unclear understanding of human intellectual abilities and the lack of an uncontroversial framework within which such understanding might be achieved. The academic study of human psychology is divided into factions that do not agree on basic methodological questions or on the definition of basic terms. The purpose of this chapter is not to be critical of human psychology, but simply to observe that it is not nor likely to be for some time, in a position to provide AI with the theoretical basis that would turn it from a form of research into a form of engineering.

In various other places (Yazdani and Whitby 1987, Whitby 1988) an analogy has been developed between AI and artificial flight. One feature of this analogy relevant here is the way in which direct imitation of natural flight proved a relatively fruitless avenue of research. It is true that many serious aviation pioneers did make detailed study of bird flight, the most notable being Otto Lilienthal; but it must be stressed that working aircraft were developed by achieving greater understanding of the principles of aerodynamics. The Wright brothers were extremely thorough and precise scientists. They succeeded because they were thorough in their experimental methods, whereas others had failed because they were too hasty to build aircraft based upon incomplete theoretical work. There may be some important lessons for AI research in the methodology of the Wrights[2].

It is also true that our understanding of bird flight has stemmed from our knowledge of aerodynamics and not the reverse[3]. If there were an imitation game type of test for flight we would probably still not be able to build a machine that could pass it. Some aircraft can imitate some features of bird flight such as a glider when soaring in a thermal, but totally convincing imitation does not exist. We do not know how to build a practical ornithopter (an aircraft that employs a birdlike wing-flapping motion), but this is not of any real importance. Some of the purposes for which we use artificial flight, such as the speedy crossing of large distances, are similar to the purposes for which natural flight has evolved, but others, such as controlling the re-entry of spacecraft, are radically different. It is clear that AI, if it is to be a useful technology, should undergo a similar development. Many of the most useful applications for AI are, and will continue to be, in areas that in no way replace or imitate natural intelligence. It is quite probable that we will never build a machine which could pass the Turing test in its entirety, but this may well be because we can see little use for such a machine, indeed it could have dangerous side-effects.

What is needed is a definition of intelligence that does not draw on our assumed intuitive knowledge of our own abilities. Such knowledge is at best vague and unreliable, and there may be Godel-like reasons for believing that we do not fully understand our own capabilities (Lucas 1961). Some writers have made tentative approaches to such a definition (Schank 1986, Yazdani 1990) and perhaps some common features are beginning to emerge, among which are that any intelligent entity must be able to form clearly discernible goals. This is a feature that is not suggested by the Turing test nor possessed by programs that have reputedly done well in the imitation game, such as: ELIZA, DOCTOR (Michie 1986), and PARRY (Colby et. al. 1972).

In considering AI as an engineering enterprise - concerned with the development of useful products - the effects of the imitation game are different but equally misleading. If we focus future work in AI on the imitation of human abilities, such as might be required to succeed in the imitation game, we are in effect building intellectual statue' when what we need are intellectual tools. This may prove to be an expensive piece of vanity. In other words, there is no reason why successful AI products should relate to us as if they were humans. They may instead resemble a workbench that enables a human operator to achieve much more than he could without it, or perhaps be largely invisible to humans in that they operate automatically and autonomously.

A More Useful Interpretation of Computing Machinery and Intelligence

If we are not to read Turing's 1950 paper as providing an operational definition of intelligence, what are we to make of it? There has, of course, been a preponderance of interpretations that stress the use of the imitation game as a test for intelligence or the ability to think. In fact, in the reported discussions about his work in the all-too-brief three years before his death in 1953 Turing seems to have to allowed this sort of interpretation to have played a significant part (Hodges 1983). Turing's toleration of such interpretations of the paper can be explained as something more than the desire for a good argument.

There is little point in being sidetracked into a discussion of Turing's actual intention at the time of his writing. This is probably correctly known in literary criticism as 'the intentionalist fallacy'. What matters is the way in which the paper has been, and is to be, interpreted. However, in order to explain the first part of a better interpretation, it is necessary to set the paper in its historical context. The 1950 paper was in many ways based upon a report written for the National Physics Laboratory in August 1948[4]. This in turn, although ostensibly a technical report, drew together Turing's speculations on the possibility of building an intelligent machine that had been carried on in conversation at least as far back as 1940 at Bletchley Park.

During this period Turing (among others) was leading what Thomas Kuhn has christened a 'paradigm shift'(Kuhn 1970). This involved an understanding of what we would now call the logical and physical aspects of certain types of systems. The wartime work at Bletchley Park was crucial to the development of this paradigm shift as Turing was one of the few men who could fully appreciate what the Polish cryptanalysts had done in the years immediately preceding 1939 in discovering how the physical nature of the Enigma coding machine could be deduced from the logical nature of its output. This work also involved the building of further physical machines such as the Colossi to assist in the deciphering of the intercepted traffic, that is the logical output of another machine. The whole of computing is founded upon this understanding of the way in which physical and logical systems can be direct counterparts of each other. However, the fact that we all understand this now should not distract us from the fact that in 1940 only a few men of vision were capable of appreciating its importance. By 1950 this paradigm shift had spread more widely in computing and the sciences, but not to philosophy or the general public.

Thus a crucial part of Computing Machinery and Intelligence is devoted to pursuing the philosophical implications of applying this paradigm shift to the question of whether or not machines can think. In the imitation game, Turing picks a man and a woman because they would be obviously physically different. Turing assumes that the general public would have no difficulty in appreciating that there are physical differences between participants in the imitation game. However the observer is denied any access to the physical attributes of the participants in the imitation game and instead must try to deduce these from their logical output via a teletype. In a way it is Enigma revisited, but with human beings. Just as the war-time cryptanalists had to deduce the physical nature of the Enigma coding device by observing logical patterns in its output, so the observer in the imitation game must attempt to distinguish the physical differences between the participants by discerning differing patterns of output.

When a machine is introduced into the game the observer is again forced to view it in terms of its logical output. Turing does not need to take a view on how successful the observer might be in distinguishing the man from the woman. He simply suggests that when a machine is introduced into the game and achieves comparable levels of success in producing indistinguishable output then we can no longer attach much importance to physical differences between women, men and machines. What Turing managed creatively to show was that the paradigm shift in which he had a leading role could be applied to the familiar question, 'Can a machine think?'. The imitation game contrived a method, understandable to a wide audience, of showing what Turing and a few others had already clearly grasped: that observable physical features have a subordinate role in answering such questions.

The remaining portion of a useful interpretation of Computing Machinery and Intelligence is more relevant today. It also explains the continuing appeal of the Turing test to present day writers. This is because the paper clearly illustrates the importance of human attitudes in determining the answers to questions such as 'Could a machine think?'.

Ascribing the label 'intelligent' is not a purely technical exercise; it involves a number of moral and social dimensions. Human beings consider themselves obligated to behave in certain ways toward intelligent items.

To claim that the ascription of intelligence has moral and social dimensions is not merely to claim that it has moral and social consequences. It may well be the case that certain moral and social criteria must be satisfied before such an ascription can be made[5]. In a sense it is true that we feel more at ease ascribing intelligence (and sometimes even the ability to think) to those entities with which we can have an interesting conversation than to radically different entities. This feature of intelligence ascription makes the use of any sort of operational test of intelligence with human beings very unattractive.

These moral and social dimensions to the ascription of intelligence are also covered by Computing Machinery and Intelligence. Turing wanted to ask (although he obviously could not answer), 'What would be the human reaction to the sort of machine that could succeed in the imitation game?'. If, as Turing clearly believed, digital computers could, by the end of the century, succeed in deceiving an interrogator 70 percent of the time, how would we describe such a feat? This is not primarily a technical or philosophical question, but rather a question about human attitudes. As Turing himself observed, the meaning of words such 'thinking' can change with changing patterns of usage. Although sampling human attitudes is rejected as a method of answering the question 'Can a machine think?' in the first paragraph of Computing Machinery and Intelligence, we can read the entire paper as primarily concerned with human attitudes. The contrivance of the imitation game was intended to show the importance of human attitudes, not to be an operational definition of intelligence.

Given this interpretation of the paper, it is not surprising that Turing tolerated a certain amount of misinterpretation of the role of the imitation game. The paper itself was partly an exercise in testing and changing human attitudes. Turing fully expected it to provoke a certain amount of controversy. However, in the fourth decade of research in AI this sort of controversy is no longer productive.

Conclusions

After the passage of forty-five years it is safe to assume that not only will Turing's prediction of machines succeeding in the imitation game by the end of the century not come about, but also that it will probably never be achieved. There would be little practical use for a machine aimed specifically at success in the imitation game. Furthermore, examination of AI products from a 1990s perspective prompts a high degree of cynicism about the possibility of success in the imitation game being simply an emergent property of computers with sufficient memory and performance.

It should be clear that at this stage in the development of AI there is nothing to be gained by clinging to the notion of the imitation game as an operational test for intelligence. It is now clear that we need AI for a number of practical purposes including the development of computing machinery towards being more useful. To imagine, for whatever reason, that this involves making computers more like human beings may well be a distracting vanity.

In conclusion it is worth repeating that the last thing needed by AI *qua* science is an operational definition of intelligence involving some sort of comparison with human beings. A Philosopher might argue that passing the Turing test, although inappropriate as an operational definition, and in no sense a sufficient condition for intelligence, is nonetheless a necessary condition of intelligence. That is to say that if we were to succeed by whatever means to produce a truly intelligent artefact, and to establish our success at this by some other set of tests, then that artefact would, of necessity, be able to pass the Turing test. There seems no good reason to believe even this weak justification for the test. Were this justification true we would would be prepared to use passing or failing the Turing test as a criterion for general intelligence in human beings. One of the main reasons that we do not is the obvious validity in this case of French's observations that the Turing test does not test for general intelligence, but for cultural similarity (French 1996). Indeed it has been persuasively argued by Bringsjord (Bringsjord 1995) that neither the Turing test, nor any proposed derivative of it, nor any foreseeable derivative of it is capable of testing for the sort of inner life or consciousness in which philosophers are interested.

The clear need in AI *qua* science is for an account of intelligence which makes no direct reference to either humans or machines. This is analogous to to the account provided by the science of aerodynamics in the field of artificial flight. AI qua engineering should not be distracted into direct copying of human performance and methods. There is no reason to assume that this is either an easy task, nor that it is likely to produce useful products.

Notes

This chapter is based upon a paper presented at the Turing 1990 Colloquium

1. The (somewhat arbitrary) dates in this history are derived from the first publications describing ELIZA (Weizenbaum 1966) and PARRY (Colby et al 1972) and the Turing 1990 Colloquium.

2. There are two features of the Wrights' methodology which contrast sharply with other contemporary experimenters and which may have relevance to contemporary AI. First they spent a good deal of time looking at the work, both successful and unsuccessful of previous aviation experimenters. They developed a coherent account of these successes and failures. Second and remarkably, unlike most of their contemporaries they had a full appreciation of the need to control any aircraft in flight addition to simply getting it airborne. (Mondey 1977)

3. In 1928 the first successful soaring flight was made in a glider; the aircraft climbing in the rising air of a thermal. Birds had been observed doing so for centuries, but at this time many biologists maintained that they could do so by virtue of the air trapped within the hollow bones of their wings being expanded by the heat of the sun. In this case a young pilot was able to overturn biological theory.

4. Eventually published (though perhaps incorrectly dated) in Meltzer, B. & Michie, D. (eds.) Machine Intelligence 5, Edinburgh University Press.

5. This should not be read as a claim that the ascription of intelligence to some entity should be made purely according to moral or social criteria. This is an interesting problem which deserves further attention. For a discussion of this issue see Torrance 1986.

References

Bringsjord, S. (1995) Could, How Could We Tell if, and Why Should - Androids Have Inner Lives, in Ford, K. , Glymour C. and Hayes, P.J. (eds) Android Epistemology, Cambridge Ma., MIT Press, pp.93-121.

Colby, K.M., Hilf, F.D., Sylvia Weber, and Kraemer, H.C. (1972) Turing-Like Indistinguishability Tests for the Validation of a Computer Simulation of Paranoid Processes in A.I., 3 (1972) pp199-222.

French, R. (1996) in Clark, A. and Millican, P. (eds) Essays in Honour of Alan Turing, O.U.P. (in press)

Hodges, A. (1983) Alan Turing , The Enigma of Intelligence, London, Unwin, pp.413-446.

Lucas, J.R. (1961) 'Minds Machines and Godel' in Philosophy Vol. XXXVI pp. 112-27.

Kuhn, T.S. (1970) The Structure of Scientific Revolutions, (2nd ed.), University of Chicago Press. Mondey, D. (ed)(1977)The International Encyclopaedia of Aviation, Octopus, London pp. 38-49.

Michie. D. (1986) On Machine Intelligence (2nd ed.), Chichester, Ellis Horwood, pp. 241-2.

Michie, D. (1996) in Clark, A. and Millican, P. (eds) Essays in Honour of Alan Turing, O.U.P. (in press)

Schank, R.C. (1986) Explanation Patterns, Lawrence Erlbaum, London.

Torrance, S. (1986), Ethics Mind and Artifice in Artificial Intelligence for Society Gill, K.S. (ed), Chichester, John Wiley and Sons, pp. 65-71

Turing, A.M.(1950) 'Computing Machinery and Intelligence', Mind, vol.LIX, No. 236. pp.433-460 .

Weizenbaum, J. (1966), 'ELIZA - A Computer Program For the Study of Natural Language Communication Between Man and Machine' Communications of the A.C.M. , vol.9 no.1 pp.36-45.

Whitby, B.R. (1988) AI: A Handbook of Professionalism Ellis Horwood, Chichester, pp.11-23 and Chapter 2.

Yazdani, M. and Whitby, B.R.(1987) 'Artificial Intelligence: Building Birds out of Beer Cans Robotica 5 pp. 89-92

Yazdani, M. (1986) in Yazdani, M. (ed) Artificial Intelligence, London, Chapman and Hall, p.263.

AI and the Law: Learning to speak each other's language

The interface of AI and the Law is a most interesting development for all involved. In addition to the technical problems that have to be solved, there will be an interchange of ideas and methodologies. As in several other areas, the indirect influence of AI will be to prompt legal professionals to examine new methodologies and consider new possibilities.

Influence will also take effect in the reverse direction. That is to say that in order to build systems that are useful to the legal profession, AI professionals will have to examine some of their most basic working assumptions. For example, legal applications may necessitate a re-examination of what McDermott has called the 'logicist' position in AI. In addition, debate has already started on the exact implications of the claim that the work of the legal profession is a rule-based activity.

Both directions of influence are, in the long-term, beneficial for both AI research and the theory of jurisprudence. However, they also entail the conclusion that it will probably not be easy to build useful AI-based legal systems in the immediate future.

Introduction

AI is not simply a technology. It is a group of ideas and innovations in methodologies, and has had far more influence at this level than it has by its introduction of working technological applications. AI has been a sufficiently powerful group of ideas to often significantly alter the domains to which it has been applied. Therefore it is likely to prompt certain methodological changes in the law. On the other hand, successful applications will only be found when AI professionals adapt to the realities of the legal application area. A crucial feature of AI in legal applications is the way in which it involves a complex interaction between two bodies of professionals.

The two-way interaction in legal applications of AI should be both more fruitful and more challenging than in other application areas. In order to interact successfully, both AI researchers and legal experts will be forced to examine some of their more basic methodological assumptions. The hope is that a process of compromise will start. This should entail building upon the expertise of a wide range of professionals in the legal area, rather than the imposition of technology-based solutions from outside.

In terms of the overall social implications of AI, the process of compromise in the legal area should force consideration of the most basic questions about the need for human participation in certain types of decision making. Whereas those with an engineering outlook may tend to assume that consistency in certain types of legal decision making is a virtue, it may be that a certain amount of inconsistency is desirable, perhaps introducing an element of humanity into this sort of decision making. There is no overwhelming case for a general answer to such questions. However, it is important that these sorts of issues are given full consideration by the legal profession, and maybe the general public, instead of being prejudged by AI researchers or decided on grounds of technological expediency alone.

Creeping AI

The effect of AI on the law will be more subtle than dramatic. Although there will be many novel technical problems for AI researchers and many interesting and lucrative cases for the legal profession, there will, more importantly, be a substantial interchange of ideas and methodologies. If the effect of AI upon jurisprudence is similar to its effect upon other disciplines and activities, this interchange of ideas will be the major way in which AI affects jurisprudence.

It has been characteristic of the development of AI that it has proved more influential in changing the ways in which other disciplines consider certain problems than through the development of working products. The major example is (perhaps paradoxically) psychology (Boden 1986). Another often quoted example is philosophy (Sloman 1978), though we might also justifiably add biology, engineering and linguistics. There can be little doubt but that AI will have a similar influence upon the area of jurisprudence. It is this pattern of influence upon methodology that forms the first and most subtle part of creeping AI.

The second tendency that justifies the label is the tendency of AI to produce small non-revolutionary improvements to computer technology, rather than a whole new type of system. In other words AI research has tended to lead to the 'filtering down' of certain computing techniques such as timesharing[1] or the use of LOGO[2] in schools. Of course, it is extremely dangerous to assume that the future will resemble the past, and this trend may suddenly change. However, all the contemporary indications are that AI will continue in this trend, rather than produce some sudden revolutionary advance.

It is necessary to labour this point somewhat because discussions of AI often suggest a very different pattern of influence. To talk of 'Fifth Generation computers' gives the impression that we are about to see a completely different type of computing machinery. The present course of AI research suggests that this is not likely to be the case. In discussing the interface of AI and the law, therefore, we are not discussing the problems of assimilating a revolutionary new technology. We are instead, primarily discussing the problems generated by the many new ideas that the AI paradigm has already spread to many other areas. This also entails that consideration of the social implications of AI developments in law should not wait upon successful applications. These may be neither so visible, nor so socially important, as the spread of ideas from AI. Attention to the sort of ideas that are introduced from technologically-based areas such as AI is important because it represents a potential set of changes in legal practices that are being driven by technology and technologists and not subject to public examination or debate. The primary responsibility for attention to this important set of ideas must lie with the legal profession, aided, if necessary, by the legislature. However, AI researchers also need to behave responsibly and not to try to introduce AI technology and methodology into the legal area without due consideration of its wider social and legal implications.

What AI has done in psychology, linguistics, biology and engineering is to bring about the consideration of different types of problem; to suggest new possibilities; to provide new analogies and methodologies. It is highly likely that AI will have the same sort of impact on jurisprudence and legal theory. Among the new possibilities that AI research has suggested is that of non-human agency in areas which were previously considered the sole preserve of human beings. An initial approach to the way in which this possibility might affect legal thinking is suggested in the next section, under the heading 'human control and agency'.

Partly as a justification of the comments made about a two-way interaction between AI and the law, the subsequent section attempts to develop some constructive features out of contemporary debates about legal applications of AI, under the heading Logicism and Rule-based Analyses. There will probably be other important, unforeseen methodological developments stimulated by the interaction between AI professionals and legal professionals. This chapter attempts to focus on just two issues that are already becoming important in the dialogue between AI researchers and legal professionals.

It is also worth remarking that these issues are not problems that have emerged in an apparently random way. They are both related products of an interaction of ideas and methodologies between AI and the law. Although both have great significance for AI applications in other areas, it may well be that the debate progresses within legal applications of AI, for reasons which are made clear below. As in other places in the book, a rather positive view has been taken here of debates that others have regarded as sometimes hostile, but that seems no bad thing.

The Social Implications of the use of AI in Law

1) Issues of Human Control and Agency

One of the most important ways in which AI has influenced other disciplines is to force them to consider the possibility of non-human agencies performing tasks which had hitherto been performed only by human beings. It is important to stress that these have rarely been immediate practical possibilities. The development of machines that can emulate or replace humans beings outside of a few, highly circumscribed, areas, has proved extremely difficult. It is also true that AI has proceeded rather more slowly towards its declared goals than most of its proponents expected. In fact, successful applications of AI are more likely to augment human intelligence than to replace it, for fairly mundane commercial and safety reasons (Whitby 1988).

In view of what was said in the previous section about the ideas suggested by AI often being more important than practical working systems, the likelihood of augmentation rather than replacement should not prevent us discussing the issues raised by the possibility of replacement. There may be lessons to be learned from the attempt to delineate those cases in the legal sphere in which we could envision the replacement of human beings by some sort of AI system.

An important aspect of this problem concerns the degree to which we wish to replace humans on performance grounds alone. In many fields there are clear technical arguments that can be made for 'taking the human out of the loop'. An example might be the control of chemical or nuclear plant where operator error increases inefficiency and the risk of accident. If an automatic device, perhaps including AI, can be shown to perform more reliably than a human operator, then the introduction of such a device would be justified on grounds of efficiency and safety. Evidence available from the fields of air and rail transport strongly indicates that devices such as Autoland 3 and driverless trains are safer than those that rely on direct human control.

Opposition to this trend is generally based on the claim that human operators can bring something extra to their work[4]. There is however a further objection to the replacement of humans in certain activities. For what might be loosely called moral reasons, there are some roles which we would want to be filled only human beings. This would be the case irrespective of whether or not human beings offered the most efficient and safest performance in that role.

An example developed in another context is the question as to whether or not we should entrust the control of strategic weapon systems completely to non-human entities such as AI programs (Yazdani and Whitby 1987, Whitby 1988).

To put it bluntly, if human beings are inclined to destroy themselves then perhaps they should reserve the right to take that decision for themselves and not to entrust it to any sort of computer system. The arguments in favour of preserving the human element in this sort of decision stems not from any consideration of decision-making ability but from the importance of the decision to humanity. Some people might take the opposite viewpoint and much prefer the presumed impartiality and consistency of AI systems over human performance. What is important is that this question is more about humanity than it is about technology and should be debated as such.

In the legal sphere there are several roles where it seems fairly clear that they should be filled only by human beings. The principle that one should be tried by one's peers, for example, would preclude the use of computer systems in establishing the guilt or innocence of a defendant. This principle might be held to stand irrespective of whether or not computers were quicker, more consistent or more impartial than human beings in the task of determining guilt or innocence. There is likely to be little objection to the principle of maintaining human control and agency in most such roles. It should be noted that simply raising the possibility has opened the debate on the extent to which we require impartiality and consistency in such decisions and the extent to which we require humanity. This AI-raised debate is not a new one in the legal sphere, but the fact that legal professionals may have responses on the importance of humanity does not mean that such responses are readily available to AI researchers.

On the other hand, there are also some less clear-cut cases where human input might be held to be desirable, but which cannot be so uncontroversially defended on the grounds that these are tasks that only humans should perform. These include the giving of legal advice and the interpretation of statute and case law. AI systems already give advice in many domains and it might seem likely that his could easily be extended to legal advice. Similarly, the introduction of AI into roles such as providing an intelligent front end for the LEXIS[5] system will gradually introduce the notion of AI having an interpretive role. The question of interpretation is highly significant, as one of the arguments discussed in the next section is that the law cannot exist in an uninterpreted form. It might be preferred, therefore, from the outset to draw the knowledge base of a legal expert system from a declared interpretation of the law, rather than the law itself.There are various systems under development, but it is probable that such systems will meet with opposition in practice. Much of this opposition may appear to be ill-informed, but the more constructive criticism may highlight the problems discussed in the next section. It seems that there are important problems underlying the development of such systems and that the ability to deal with them could represent an important step forward for AI.

2) What sort of AI, What sort of Law?

An interesting criticism which has been made of AI methodology is the challenge to what McDermott has has called the 'logicist' position in AI (McDermott 1987). McDermott's central objection to logicism is that it contains the hidden premise that a significant amount of thought is deductive. McDermott feels that this hidden premise cannot be maintained. This is probably not the place to attempt to resolve this debate. However, if AI is proceeding under this methodological assumption we can expect it to be challenged in the legal sphere.

The questions and possibilities raised by consideration of logicism in AI methodology are paralleled in jurisprudential theory by the debates surrounding legal positivism 6. To consider in detail the relationship between these two approaches would be inappropriate here and it would be simplistic to argue that they are exact counterparts of each other. However, it can be observed that if the use of AI in law is entirely under both the requirements of of logicism and legal positivism then there may be serious problems generated.

Put simply, these problems stem from the fact that both logicism and legal positivism are still controversial and it is by no means clear that all the requirements of the correct use of AI in law can be captured by these two methodological assumptions. This is not only an abstract theoretical point. If systems are built and introduced under these methodological assumptions, then legal practice will have been significantly altered by technological requirements alone. Since legal practice should ultimately serve human rather than technological requirements, these issues should be decided by some sort of human consensus and not by technological expediency. There seem to be very strong arguments in favour of a requirement for additional considerations above those of technological expediency in the use of AI in law. An attempt will be made to clarify this in the rest of this chapter.

It should be remembered that it will not be sufficient in practice to give merely theoretical consideration to these arguments. More positive measures will be required since it will probably always be easiest to build AI systems under one or both of the assumptions that logicism and legal positivism capture all that needs to be done in this sphere. It may well be necessary to enforce higher standards. That is to say that informed practitioners in the areas of both AI and the law may have to take positive steps to oppose the introduction of AI systems which grossly oversimplify the problems and techniques required in this area. Ideally this would be done by something along the lines of a professional body or an 'ethical committee' composed of experts on the various issues involved.

This can be illustrated effectively by consideration of one particular technical problem involved in the building of AI systems in law. This is the question as to whether the knowledge base of a legal expert system should be based upon statute (or some formalisation of statute) or, on the other hand, upon the interpretation of statute by an experienced legal practitioner. There is, of course, a series of technical questions as to which approach will produce the most effective expert system. It should be equally clear that there is a series of moral and legal questions involved.

First, there is a problem in describing the exact legal status of such a knowledge base. If, for example, the knowledge base is primarily a direct formalization of a piece of statute by a knowledge engineer without legal qualifications, it is perhaps premature to attribute any legal status to it, even if it is designed to accessed only by qualified legal professionals. Second, there is the problem that this knowledge base represents a reification and perhaps also a freezing of one particular interpretation of statute. Future development of the interpretive process may be effectively prevented, or at the least hindered, by the existence of such a knowledge base. This tendency can be seen in various ways: as either desirable or dangerous or both or neither. What is important about this tendency, however, is that it too represents a subordination of matters that should rightly be matters of public debate, to matters of technological expediency.

This problem is particularly acute in applications where a system is envisaged to assist in the administration of statute or of administrative law. In such applications the use of AI in law may represent a serious increase in the power of the executive and legislative branches of government at the expense of the judiciary. Again, there may be arguments in favour of this sort of change, but it is unlikely that technological expediency will be the most persuasive of them.

It has been argued that the law should be viewed not as an objective structured system but as a process of social negotiation or as a continuing battle between legislators and the judiciary (Leith 1986). If this argument has any validity, then it would seem that the legislators may have a potent, but unwitting ally in AI technology. If the law is regarded as being primarily a process of social negotiation, then the idea that there is one correct interpretation of statute is clearly absurd. Researchers and legal professionals attempting to introduce AI into legal applications, even in apparently mundane applications such as intelligent front ends for legal databases, will tend to increase the importance of a small range of interpretations, and perhaps frustrate the development of new interpretations.

Of course, these criticisms assume an unnecessary restriction upon the methods available for implementing AI systems in law. There is no reason inherent in AI methodology for always insisting on the primacy of deductive reasoning, though this tendency may have developed in the minds of AI researchers through exposure to rather out-of-date philosophical viewpoints. Similarly, there are many application areas and techniques which do not involve increasing the power of legislators relative to other legal functions.

Simply observing that AI methodology and practice can avoid the criticisms above does not mean that it will always do so. What is much easier is to concentrate on deductive reasoning and to make the assumption that there are clear rules or, even worse, to pay lip service to other methodological approaches, but actually to build systems using simplifying assumptions such as these. To counter such tendencies the critical input of the legal profession will be essential.

Avoiding the criticisms above has brought us back to the issue of human control and agency. If we have to accept a view of the law as always interpreted, or even as a process of social negotiation, then the role of an AI system, even just as a front end to LEXIS, is arguably a social role. At the very least AI is replacing humans in the role of interpretation. This replacement may be important, partly for the lack of humanity discussed in the last section, and also because of the ways use of AI-based systems can legitimate, and make more rigid, the body of knowledge that they present. Interpretation by AI and by humans cannot be identical because humans tend to react differently to each type of interpreter. Thus even in what seems to be a purely technical use of AI in law we run into problems of human control and agency, if the law is seen as principally a process of social negotiation, rather than a formal code.

The exact method of achieving working AI systems in law also raises the sort of problem discussed in the last section. For example, Susskind puts the balance of change towards jurisprudential changes, suggesting that knowledge engineers will help to produce an 'interpretive legal science' (Susskind 1987). If it is jurisprudence, rather than AI that has to change, then the very process of introducing AI is correctly seen as a legal process and perhaps also a social change. However, it can also be argued that AI could change, perhaps along the lines described above. In the end it is likely that both areas will change. These changes cannot be avoided, because of the influence of creeping AI, but they would clearly seem to require both legal and social scrutiny.

Conclusions

AI is likely to have a far more subtle influence on the law and legal practice than would be expected were it to be regarded as merely a new technology. AI is much more than a technology, it represents powerful new methods of looking at familiar problems. Because of this, the legal profession must develop a coherent and useful response to AI and its philosophical underpinning. This is both a novel and an urgent task. If the initiative is left with the proponents of AI then legal practice may be irrevocably changed, at the very least, in some of the ways suggested in this and the next chapter.

Of course, it may be that such changes will be considered a great improvement. I have argued at length elsewhere (Whitby 1988) that enthusiasm for what AI can do may be fuelled more by cynicism about human abilities and tendencies than by the real possibilities of the technology. It is hoped that the notion that human beings ought generally to be replaced in the field of legal practice will be open to serious and informed debate. The role of the human being as interpreter and decision-maker in law, as in so many other fields, will have to be re-examined. Re-examination, however, need not entail devaluation, delimitation or deprecation.

That is to say that there are clearly two possible points of view on the issue of human control and agency mentioned above. If one believes that the human decision maker or interpreter in the legal area exists purely to achieve some further goal, such as consistency or impartiality, then one will be unable to counter arguments from proponents of AI who can claim that these goals will be better achieved by the use of non-human devices such as AI. On the other hand, if one believes that the human decision maker or interpreter contributes something to the legal process simply by being human, then one is likely to resist any change which appears to threaten the role of the human decision maker or interpreter.

There may be passionate divisions of opinion over this issue and there is little time in which to develop the debate before the introduction of working systems begins to pre-empt discussion of implications. The involvement of the legal profession in discussion of these matters is vitally important.

Legal professionals therefore need to develop a response to the introduction of AI that is:

1) Not Luddite. Little will be gained by the delay or denial of the new possibilities raised by developments in AI.
2) Constructive. That is, inclined to build upon these possibilities, rather than just to criticise. It should be clear that theoreticians from the legal sphere can make a contribution to the philosophical foundations of AI in areas such as the debate on logicism.
3) Balanced. That is, neither over-enthusiastic about new technology because of the perceived limitations of humans, nor set against it for equally irrational reasons.

A useful first step might be the introduction of something along the lines of an ethical committee that could consider some of the legal, social and political implications of AI systems in law which present special problems. The criteria for membership of such a committee are by no means clear, but almost any committee would be more effective and carry more consensus than the present reliance on ad hoc decisions, often by researchers with limited legal knowledge and without public scrutiny or debate. The speed at which technological changes can occur makes it essential that the legal profession take an immediate interest in this sort of problem.

AI professionals, on the other hand, will have to acknowledge the importance of the contribution of experienced practitioners in changing their own methodological assumptions. It is important to remember that the methods of working in an application area, such as the law, form a significant proportion of the knowledge of that area. It is not always appropriate,therefore, to simplify or alter such techniques in order to render the area suitable for the introduction of AI. If simplifying assumptions are introduced in order to build a working program, there clearly will come a point at which experts in the application area will rightly feel that the program is no longer dealing with real problems, but rather with oversimplified pseudo-problems.

Notes

1. Timesharing is a commonly-used technique for organizing the operating system of any computer to attend to several tasks and or users simultaneously which originated in early AI work. Nowadays it would be regarded as part of general computer science, not AI.

2. LOGO is an educational computer language, very commonly found in schools that was originally developed by Seymour Papert - an AI researcher - though most of the teachers using LOGO would not associate it with AI.

3. Autoland is a system that provides fully automatic control of airliners during the approach and landing. It has been employed at many major international airports for over 15 years during which time it has achieved an excellent safety record. The only reportable incidents in the use of this system have been caused by pilots mistakenly taking control away from Autoland.

4. These extra items are often claimed to be common sense, creativity, and intuition.

5. LEXIS is the main legal database now in everyday use by much of the legal profession in Britain. LEXIS Handbook, 1981.

6. Legal Positivism is a view of the nature of law as fully described by a set of rules, stemming ultimately from the legitimate authority in a community. There are problems with this view of the nature of law, some of which are directly relevant to the construction of AI systems in law. (von der Leith Gardner, 1984)

References

Boden, M.A. (1986) Artificial Intelligence and Natural Man, Boston, MIT Press.

Leith, P. (1986) Fundamental Errors in Legal Logic Programming, The Computer Journal 29,6.

von der Leith Gardner, A. (1984), An Artificial Intelligence Approach to Legal Reasoning dissertation published by Dept. of Comp. Science, Stanford University esp pp.24-25.

LEXIS Handbook, 1981, London, Butterworth Telepublishing.

McDermott, D.A. (1987) A Critique of Pure Reason, Computational Intelligence.

Sloman (1978) The Computer Revolution in Philosophy, Brighton, Harvester.

Susskind, R.E. (1987) Expert Systems in Law, Oxford, Clarendon Press.

Whitby, B.(1988), AI: A Handbook of Professionalism, Chichester, Ellis Horwood. esp. ch.1 and pp.103-128.

Yazdani, M and Whitby, B (1987) Accidental Nuclear War, the Contribution of AI in AI Review 1, 3, 1897.

AI and the Law: Proceed with Caution

Introduction

There can be little doubt that the law is an attractive application area for AI. Not only is the law already becoming an important and lucrative area for computing in general, but it has a number of features that make AI techniques in particular appear useful and interesting.

First, it is an area that often involves working with very large amounts of data. The sheer quantity of text that has to be searched in order to find relevant judgements suggests an application for computer-based techniques of effective search. Secondly this data is very often mixed with knowledge and any search algorithm is therefore required to accommodate an interpretive element. That is to say that present 'brute force' computing techniques such as simple matching of keywords may not be able to produce the most effective search because they lack any ability to handle the sense of the text. AI techniques that seek to provide this ability would find welcome applications in the legal area. Consider for example, the task of using a computer to search for relevant precedents. In the case of the use of a 'brute force' keyword search this requires the user to be relatively imaginative in choosing a keyword and to perform all the work of ascertaining the meaning of the text. AI research is directed at helping in this task in two ways. There are techniques that could enable the user to be more productively vague in telling the system for what to search. Similarly, there are techniques that might enable the system to search for patterns or scenarios that are closer to relevant precedents than keywords are.

With the increasing use of computers in all manner of areas, there will inevitably be more use of, and contact with, computers by the legal profession. This, in turn, will generate a need for legal databases such as LEXIS[1] to adopt AI techniques in order both to perform more effective searches than the present 'keyword' techniques permit, and to make the human interface more generally useful. In both these areas, AI research has some useful techniques to offer and inevitably there will be others. The present generation of expert systems, although crude, are sufficient to provide advice giving systems, many of which will find employment somewhere within the legal area. Small improvements to such advice-giving systems are taking place constantly, so it would be unwise to dismiss this technology on the basis of present-day products.

These developments bring in their wake a number of interesting technical questions. Some of these will be concerned with the degree to which certain types of human judgement can be formalised. Although AI has, in general, had only limited success in formalizing human judgement, this is a central focus of AI research. In the legal sphere, it is reasonable to expect that research will continue that may lead to the formalisation of some types of legal judgement.

It is also important to remark at this stage that the main influence of AI in the legal area is likely to be through the importation of ideas and methodologies rather than working technology. That is to say that it will be some time before it is reasonable to expect that AI-based systems will do a significant amount of the work in the legal area. On the other hand, there is already an important osmosis of ideas from AI to many other disciplines (including jurisprudence).

Even when AI is assessed as a technology it has tended to produce a series of improvements to existing technology, rather than revolutionary advances. In most of its application areas, AI research has tended to lead to the 'filtering down' of certain computing techniques such as timesharing[2] or the use of LOGO[3] in schools. It is just possible that a sudden revolutionary advance will thrust intelligent machines into the legal area, but all indications are that this is unlikely. Probably, AI will continue to produce relatively small technical improvements rather than some sudden revolutionary advance.

What is under consideration here, therefore, is not the consequences of the widespread use of intelligent systems in the legal area. It is instead a more relevant and realistic consideration of the many small changes in outlook and methodology AI will produce in the legal area.

It is, of course, difficult at this stage to provide any detailed forecast of the sort of methodological changes in jurisprudence and legal practice that might be started by an exposure to the methods of AI. Some suggestions that have been made include reconsideration of legal positivist arguments and re-examination of the possibility of recognising non-human control and agency in some spheres of activity (chapter 4, Whitby 1990).

This chapter takes a more direct approach, considering the social and political changes likely to follow the methodological changes prompted by the use of AI in the legal sphere. The unfortunate conclusion drawn is that little is being done to monitor these changes and the gung-ho tradition of the computer industry gives reason for concern about such developments. The legal profession and other interested groups, therefore, must take great care to fully examine these developments and to ensure that they are generally beneficial.

This, in turn, will require that legal professionals adopt a realistic position with respect to the technologically induced changes in the legal sphere. They must reject contemptuous cynicism about the practical limitations of AI systems. As has already been stressed, the influence of AI goes far beyond its ability to deliver useful working systems. Similarly, they have little to gain from a Luddite rejection of a technology with great potential benefits. Instead they need to make a calm and serious examination of issues such as those considered in the remaining sections of this chapter. The legal profession needs to participate in attempts to develop codes of practice and software standards.

One product of the fuller interaction between the legal profession and AI system designers should be that it will force consideration of the most basic questions about the need for human participation in certain types of decision making. That is to say that whereas those with an the outlook of an engineer may tend automatically to assume that consistency in all types of decision making is a virtue, in the legal area it may be that a certain amount of inconsistency is desirable, perhaps because it can introduce an element of humanity into legal decision making. There is no overwhelming case for a general answer to such questions. However, it is important that issues like these are given full consideration by the legal profession, and maybe the general public, instead of being prejudged by AI system builders or decided on grounds of technological expediency alone.

In examining some of the problems of the social implications of AI in law it may appear that a completely negative view is being taken: this is not the case. AI represents a collection of methodological innovations that has already proved very fruitful in the area of cognitive science. Considered as a technology, AI has the potential to produce immense social benefits. Consideration of the need for some minimal safeguards in the area of AI and the law should not prompt the rejection or needless delay of beneficial developments. What is needed is merely a certain degree of caution.

Possible Social Implications of the use of AI in Law

A significant change that AI has brought into many other disciplines is that of forcing them to consider the possibility of non-human agencies performing tasks which have previously been performed only by human beings. As remarked in the introduction, these have rarely been immediate practical possibilities, but rather possibilities for discussion. The development of machines that can emulate or replace humans beings outside of a few, highly circumscribed areas, has proved extremely difficult. It is also true that AI has proceeded rather more slowly towards its declared goals than most of its proponents expected.

Nonetheless, the fairly widespread acceptance of expert systems technology in industry has opened discussion on the possibility of replacing or removing human beings from many areas where this was previously considered impossible. Some aspects of the law and legal practice have been included in these discussions. One social implication of the use of AI in the law that has received a fair amount of attention, therefore, is the replacement of legal professionals, from secretaries to judges, by AI-based systems. For a number of reasons, discussed at length elsewhere (Whitby 1988), these are science-fiction rather than real concerns. A more realistic possibility is the introduction of expert systems to assist such legal professionals in their work.

A working party of the Council for Science and Society (Council for Science and Society 1989) identified a number of stages in the provision of expert legal help. These were identifying the client's problem, determining the applicable laws, the choice of tactics, and the prognosis of the client's case. Of these they considered the first and last stages unpromising areas for the use of expert systems. The stages of determining the applicable legislation and the choice of tactics were areas where they anticipated the use of expert systems, to assist both lawyers and 'less well qualified counsellors'.

Experience in manufacturing industry has, however, already shown that this pattern of introducing of AI-based technology, while not directly replacing human labour can lead to deskilling. That is the elimination of the highly skilled, and often expensive, content of a particular job so that it can be performed in a more routine manner, and often by cheaper employees or computer systems. A process of deskilling could well be seen in the introduction of AI technology to legal theory and practice.

One pattern of deskilling in industry has been the drastic reduction, or elimination of skill-based jobs in manufacturing. For example computer-numerically-controlled (CNC) technology has enabled designers to produce their designs directly, without the need for skilled turners and machinists on the shop floor. Many contemporary computer-assisted design and computer-assisted manufacture (CAD-CAM) systems allow a product to be designed on a computer screen and then directly transmitted in order to be physically produced on a computer controlled machine. Manufacturing still needs a relatively small number of designers and a larger number of lower paid workers to pack and deliver its products.

A process analogous to this pattern of deskilling in manufacturing may well take place in the legal area. There, the designers are in a sense the legislators, and the skilled turners and machinists can be seen as members of the judiciary - those who interpret and enforce legislation. Just as the managers of manufacturing industry found advantages in removing the process of human interpretation in product design where this was technologically possible, so the legislature (those who frame and enact legislation) may find it advantageous to reduce the process of human interpretation of legislation to the extent that this is technologically possible. The potential to reduce the importance of human interpretation of the law may not be obvious. However, this is something that is not only possible but which may already be taking place. An example is provided by the introduction of the DSS (Department of Social Security) Local Office Demonstrator (Browne and Taylor 1989).

The Local Office Demonstrator is a decision support system, built on expert system principles, that is intended to help in the adjudication of eligibility for income support (Social Security) payments. It is based upon a logical model of the relevant legislation. This sort of system may be accurately described as being within existing AI capabilities. Browne and Taylor, however, point out a number of dangers that a naive approach to this area can bring. In particular, a number of organisational choices have to be made about how the system will be used and for whose benefit. They feel that the designers of systems such as the Local Office Demonstrator may produce systems with four main types of failing. First, they may mislead the user as to the status of knowledge contained in the system. Second, they may threaten the responsibility of the individual decision maker, thereby undermining the network of political and social responsibilities on which that responsibility is based. Third, they may be introduced in a way that deskills those involved with the system, and fourthly, they may be irrelevant and difficult for the user. To a large extent, therefore, Browne and Taylor's concerns, particularly the third and fourth, parallel the organisational problems thrown up by the introduction of computer technology in manufacturing industry discussed above.

One argument that may well be advanced in favour of the introduction of AI systems such as the Local Office Demonstrator may be that they will help to ensure a consistent interpretation of the law. Browne and Taylor make it clear that this is an important motivation in the construction of the Local Office Demonstrator. The client of the DSS may face very different decisions from different human interpreters of the relevant Social Security legislation and regulations. Superficially it may seem that if the introduction of

AI and similar technologies can increase the consistency of application of legislation then this is desirable from the point of view of the end user.

However, this superficial analysis fails to reveal the full price of greater consistency in the application of legislation. Just as in the industrial analogy, there may be less respectable reasons why those in power may wish to ensure consistency in the application of their decisions. It may be part of a process of increasing their power at the expense of those responsible for the interpretive process. One of the general effects of introducing computer technology into industry is that it enables those in charge to ensure that their decisions are carried out to the letter and not modified by various interpretations and re-interpretations as they pass down a human chain of command. AI has a significant role to play in increasing the prevalence and effectiveness of this change. In the legal area this increase in power may be extremely significant.

Philip Leith is a writer on legal logic programming who may well be dismissed by those engaged in the actual production of AI systems in law because of his outspoken hostility to the whole area. However, in an article on AI and the law (Leith 1986) he makes a point that supports the claims of this section with respect to the social implications of such systems. Leith observes that the legislature can be seen as to some extent in conflict with the judiciary. This is a view which reflects constitutional theory from the time of Montesquieu, which stresses the need for the various organs of authority in a society to act as checks on each other. This is particularly important in a country like Britain that has no written constitution explicitly limiting the powers of the various organs of government. If, as Leith claims, the legal process is principally a process of social negotiation', the introduction of AI into the legal area is likely to change this constitutional balance.

In a manner essentially similar to the sort of changes prompted in industry by the introduction of CNC and CAD-CAM technology, the introduction of AI into the legal area is almost certainly about to ensure that decisions are carried out to the letter. There are, however, reasons to be even more concerned about these problems when they are encountered in the legal area. It is vitally important in a pluralistic democracy that such constitutional changes are openly debated before they take effect. The implementation of ad hoc constitutional changes by a group of AI specialists who have no explicit understanding of their professional and social responsibilities cannot be regarded as acceptable. This point will be taken up again in the conclusions.

Social Feedthrough

The technical considerations involved in the design and production of a piece of technology have an important influence over the social implications of the general use of that technology. It is for this reason that scientists, technologists and technocrats must fully consider their social responsibilities when taking what are appear to be purely technical design decisions. This observation is as true of the use of AI in law as it is of nuclear technology, biotechnology, and pharmaceuticals. The term 'social feedthrough' is intended to signify the way in which technical decisions can produce differing social effects.

Some examples of social feedthrough have already been provided by Browne and Taylor. Of particular importance in their estimation, are decisions concerning which groups of people the system is intended to support. In the case of most AI systems these groups will fall under the heading 'users'. In a situation where there is an established, and perhaps productive, conflict of interests it is important to remember that one group typically gains at the expense of another. If we accept some part of Leith's description of the law as a process of social negotiation then the designers of sophisticated AI systems for use in the legal area are significant players in that process of social negotiation.

This may be an unpopular claim with AI researchers. The technical thrust of much AI development has rested on the assumption that most of the thinking within its application areas is logical in form. This has been called the 'logicist' position (McDermott 1987). There is a significance to the areas of law chosen for incorporation in AI systems having a fairly clear logical structure. That is to say that they tend to be portions of highly specific and circumscribed statutes. The areas of the law (and they are many) that require the resolution of ambiguities or the application of interpretive skills have so far been avoided by AI researchers. This also facilitates the avoidance of giving due consideration to questions of social consequences.

There is no doubt that the easiest parts of legal practice to incorporate in the present generations of AI systems are portions of statute with very specific reference and a clear logical structure. Even in these areas, however, it is certain that the introduction of advice systems such as the Local Office Demonstrator, or a similar system intended to advise on the British Nationality Act (1981), would have important social implications. Their widespread use would remove the need for much of the present process of human adjudication on the application of the relevant statute.

It is more than coincidence that both these examples of research into the use of AI in law contain what is known as an 'ouster clause', a clause specifically designed by the legislators to prevent the process of interpretation by the judiciary. There may be debate on the importance of such clauses among lawyers and constitutional scholars, but they remain unremarked by AI system builders. The implementation of an AI system that will help circumvent the process of judicial interpretation can achieve far more in the prevention of judicial interpretation than any ouster clause ever did. (As Leith remarks, ouster clauses have generally been ignored by the judiciary). In the implementation of public policy in areas such as the control of immigration or the adjudication of social security payments, use of an AI system can help to provide a rigid interpretation of government policy. Use of an AI system can also allow a vast reduction in the skill level of those involved in enforcing government policy at the point of contact with the general public. This is directly analogous to the way in which CAD-CAM and CNC technology has permitted deskilling, accompanied by greater control by top management in industry.

The first, and perhaps the most important example of social feedthrough, therefore, occurs in the choice of the body of legislation to be included in an AI system. If this is, like the two examples mentioned above, a piece of administrative law containing ouster clauses then it is likely that any involvement of AI systems will lead to a change in the balance of power away from the judiciary.

A second series of examples of social feedthrough is caused by assumptions about the relationship between system and user. As much of the 'pure research' component of AI has been interested in the direct imitation of certain human capabilities, there has been a tendency for applied AI to assume that it can and should replace human beings in certain jobs. There is probably a number of jobs that are so dangerous or unpleasant that no human being should be required to perform them, but few, if any, of these fall in the area of AI in law. It is, perhaps, natural in the design of an AI system to assume that it will perform in much the same way as a human might perform in a particular role. As the process of implementation continues, therefore, those responsible for the introduction of the AI system fall into a process of looking at redundancies and deskilling. This process could be avoided by not making the sort of technical assumptions that lead in this direction.

An analogous set of problems has been well described (Wenger 1987, O'Shea and Self 1983) in the area of AI in education, usually referred to as Intelligent Tutoring Systems (ITS). The early notions in this area saw the task of the teacher as holding a vast quantity of knowledge and slowly feeding it to pupils. Experience has revealed that perhaps more important than this task are other components of teaching such as diagnosing and correcting mistaken learning, providing examples, identifying difficulties, and judging the pace at which to proceed. Because of this, it has proved more appropriate to design teaching aids than automated teachers.

It is reasonable to expect that the application of AI to the legal sphere will follow a similar pattern. It will probably be more appropriate to design AI systems that perform as legal aids rather than automated lawyers, therefore. That is to say that the designer should assume from the outset that the system will be used by experienced and competent professionals. One technical way in which this design objective can be achieved has been described and demonstrated in the medical field (Miller 1984, 1986). What Miller describes are expert critiquing systems that converse with a physician about a problem in patient management. Instead of simply presenting a diagnosis, a critiquing system would ask for the physician's diagnosis and/or plan and then present a critique of that. This seems a highly appropriate technology for the introduction of AI into the legal sphere.

Further technical considerations that would be appropriate in this area stem from the notion of human-centred computing (Cooley 1987). The legal area is one in which the removal of responsibility of creativity from the user by uninformed system design may have many important social consequences. For the sort of constitutional reasons touched upon in the previous section, it is extremely important to avoid the building of AI systems that restrict the competence and creativity of legal users.

Some Conclusions

There is a series of AI-induced changes already taking place in both jurisprudence and legal practice. Although it may be difficult to predict their exact nature, there can be no doubt that significantsocial consequences will result from these changes. One of the most significant of these is the redistribution of the constitutional balance of power.

There may be those who would wish to argue that the constitutional change of removing interpretive prerogative from the judiciary is generally beneficial. They may see the activities of lawyers in interpretation of statutes as undermining legitimate authority, or wasting the time and money of citizens involved with the legal process. This a political position that requires a good deal of justification and not something which should emerge as a largely unforeseen consequence of new technologies being introduced.

The central problem with the constitutional change is that it is largely going unremarked and unnoticed: it is not yet clear which groups should monitor and control such a change. However, it would be unfortunate if such a change were simply allowed to happen. It is a change that affects all citizens to some degree, but would seem to affect the legal profession most directly. Although it were best for AI professionals to adopt higher standards and to pay more attention to some of the social consequences of their work, the central responsibility will probably be left with the legal profession.

However, because of the relationship between technical design and social consequences that we have called social feedthrough, some responsibility will fall on those engaged in designing AI systems in law and they should follow the admonitions of Browne and Taylor and the Council for Science and Society. That is to say they should avoid producing systems that deskill or threaten the responsibility of their users. In addition, we must hope that those involved with the selling and management of such systems do not give or succumb to the impression that the systems are more competent or more impartial than they really are.

Wishing is unlikely to guarantee changing the habits of an industry that tends to produce products first and consider social implications later if at all. What is required is that those involved with the design, building, and selling of such systems behave in a professional manner.

In this context 'behave in a professional manner' means taking responsibility for the impact of one's field of expertise on others and conforming to recognised good practice in one's work. Most other groups who realise their ability to influence the lives of others to any great degree place great stress on concepts of professional responsibility. In most professions this responsibility is not left to the good will of those practising the profession, but is institutionalized as in medical ethics and the like. There is little sign that AI is moving in this direction and pressure may have to applied by the legal profession to improve standards.

An example of professional behaviour, yet to appear in the field of AI, would be the publication of what is to be regarded as good practice in the design and implementation of AI systems. This would not only guide those working to produce such systems, but would be a valuable aid to the legal profession. At present, the law is without any concept of what AI is, let alone what is considered good practice in AI.

If cases come before the courts that involve AI there are no established principles on which to base judgements. There has been much discussion of the responsibility of scientists and technologists over the last decades, particularly since the development of nuclear weapons and genetic engineering which seem to raise questions as to whether individual scientists can be held responsible for the long-term consequences of their discoveries. At the same time, there has been a growing concern among scientists with respect to the social implications of their work.

This process is far from complete, but the excuse that one is just a scientist and the consequences of one's work are someone else's concern, will carry even less weight in future. The concept of professionalism in this context entails that those actually working with AI should take responsibility for the social consequences of their technological design decisions. Through a greater attention to professionalism, or through direct legal control, AI design and implementation need to take account of many factors beyond mere technological expediency.

Greater professionalism on the part of AI scientists and technologists is only part of what is required to ensure that developments in legal applications of AI are correctly monitored and controlled. The legal profession needs to take an active interest in these developments: if the designers and builders of AI systems continue to see themselves as technicians rather than professionals, then it will be necessary to bring their work under the direct control of the law. In this case, the law will require an accurate understanding of the real and potential problems arising from AI.

Although there are already a number of informal attempts on the part of AI researchers to resolve issues such as these (Computers and Social Responsibility, the Council for Science and Society, and the Journal for AI and Society), it may soon be time for a more formal co-operation between the legal profession and AI. For example an ethics committee, in spite of the lack of attractiveness of such items, would provide a source of guidance for the designers of AI systems in law. The best solution would be for all involved with AI to be fully aware of the sort of social implications discussed in this book.

It should also be remarked that there are also benefits for the legal profession in this sort of interaction. In order to be able to help in the drafting and enforcement of the growing body of legislation in this area they need to have a full and deep understanding of the technology. This would prevent knee-jerk legislation', like the Data Protection Act (1984) and the Computer Misuse Act (1990). The shape of both owes more to relatively uninformed public opinion than to detailed understanding of computer technology and the needs of those affected by it.

Of course, since everybody is affected as a citizen by such matters as changes in the constitutional balance of power and the standardization of the application of legislation, it would be as well to have general public debate on these issues.

Notes

1. LEXIS is the main legal database now in everyday use by much of the legal profession in Britain. LEXIS Handbook, Butterworth Telepublishing, London 1981.

2. Timesharing is a commonly-used technique for organizing the operating system of any computer to attend to several tasks and or users simultaneously which originated in early AI work. Nowadays it would be regarded as part of general computer technology and few remember its origins in AI research.

3. LOGO is an educational computer language, very commonly found in schools which was originally developed by Seymour Papert - an AI researcher - though most of the teachers using LOGO would not associate it with AI.

References

Browne J. and Taylor A. (1989) The Inherent Dangers of 'Naive' Legal Knowledge Bases, AISBQ 68.

Cooley, M. (1987) Architect or Bee? The Human Price of Technology, London, Hogarth Press.

Council for Science and Society (1989) Benefits and Risks of Knowledge-Based Systems, Oxford University Press.

Leith P. (1986) Fundamental errors in Legal Logic Programming, The Computer Journal, Vol 29, No. 6.

McDermott D.A. (1987) Fundamental Errors in Legal Logic Programming, Computational Intelligence

Miller P.L. (1984) A Critiquing Approach to expert Computer Advice: Attending, Boston, Ma., Pitman.

Miller P.L. (1986), Expert Critiquing Systems, New York, Springer-Verlag.

O'Shea T. and Self J. (1983) Learning and Teaching with Computers, Brighton, Harvester Press.

Wenger E. (1987) Artificial Intelligence and Tutoring Systems, Los Altos, Ca. Morgan Kaufmann.

Whitby B. (1988) Artificial Intelligence: A Handbook of Professionalism, Chichester, Ellis Horwood.

Whitby B. (1990) AI and the Law: learning to speak each other's language, in Narayanan (ed), Law, Computer Science, and Artificial Intelligence, Vol. 1, New Jersey, Ablex.

Ethical AI

As has already been observed, particularly in Chapter 2, the incautious use of anthropomorphic terminology, and the raising of excessive expectations about how much can be achieved in the near future, have all played a part in the development of AI. As earlier observed, one of the major causes of this attitude is the status attributed to the Turing test for most of the period in question. What requires exploration next is the way in which these aspects of the history of AI have detracted from the public image of AI.

In the 1980s, many highly extravagant claims were made about AI applications. Technologies like expert systems were, it seemed, about to solve most of mankind's problems. Some of the more extravagant forecasts looked towards knowledge-based solutions to war, third world poverty, and human misery in general. They predicted medical and legal expert systems that would bring access for all to the latest medical and legal knowledge. Of course, at the same time, some writers sounded a note of caution. Perhaps the extravagant predictions might bring with them certain problems. Perhaps more attention should have been paid to the fact that the number of genuine working AI applications remained small and the amount of human misery reduced by them even smaller. On balance, however, it was the AI enthusiasts who carried the day.

It would be unfair to give names in either case, but this is not so long ago. In the 1990s, there is much more cynicism and caution about the number of really successful AI applications likely to be in use this century. There has also been a significant decrease in funding for AI research in general, though the history of AI in chapter 2 suggests that funding may well increase again in another AI boom at some point in the future. Expert systems are no longer in vogue as a research topic, let alone promoted as the solution to most of mankind's problems. Those areas of AI that can still attract research funding often take considerable pains to distinguish themselves from previous approaches to AI. In some commercial organisations AI research has had to be given another name to render it acceptable.

These historical events are not unrelated. Those who not only jumped on the AI bandwagon during the 80s, but accelerated it to a ridiculous speed, and those who let them are, in part, responsible for the decline in AI during the 1990s. This decline in interest stands in need of explanation. Recession and the end of the Cold War have played their part, but the credibility of AI seems to have been damaged to a greater extent than mere economic factors could have achieved. There can be little doubt that one of the main causes is reaction to the over-optimistic forecasts of the 1980s. This would seem to suggest that this sort of excessive claim or wildly optimistic forecast is, apart from being unethical, bad for business, in the long term.

In the short-term it might seem advantageous to promise more than can be easily delivered, either to customers or to funding bodies, if one's competitors are making this sort of over-optimistic claim then the temptation is even greater. How else can one maintain a share of market or funding? In other words, general standards of responsibility start to fall. This applies equally to academic researchers and to commercial suppliers. In the world of computing in general there has been much software of lamentable quality sold. AI contributed its own special feature to this lowering of standards - the extravagant promise. Many research objectives which might have been better described as fifty-year goals were promised as five-year programmes. It is not clear whether the purveyors of unreliable software and unfulfillable promises were mistakenly trying to create more widespread interest or simply following a market trend. Eventually, of course, customers or funding bodies will realise that they are not getting what they expected. The resulting reaction is a loss of interest that affects the responsible and the irresponsible alike.

It is to guard against this sort of devaluation of a whole market area by unscrupulous sub-standard practicioners - known in Britain as cowboys - that many industries set up standards. These cover such things as product standards, standards of training and qualification, recognized good practice, and the impact on society and the environment. These may not seem to matter in the short term, as during the scramble for funding for AI in the 1980s. In the long term, however, they are essential.

The business advantages of being ethical apply not only to general product standards but also to employee relations. In the relatively closed world of AI, a disgruntled employee does not cease to exist if dismissed. He or she is almost certain to find work with a customer or competitor. The negative advertising that is likely to ensue from this will almost certainly be much more expensive than would the production of good employee relations in the first place. This process applies equally to academia. The university lecturer or researcher who falls out with unsympathetic administration will, quite probably, go to work at a competing institution where he or she will be best placed to criticise or take action against the administration that quarrelled with him or her in the first place. Responsible management will go to great lengths to prevent this sort of thing. In the long term it is, like other unethical practices, bad for business. Unethical behaviour being bad for business needs to be stressed because a culture seems to have grown up that believes ethical considerations are not relevant to hard-nosed businessmen or researchers. The following fairly outspoken comments from students' essays seem to sum this up: 'being ethical means letting your competitors take advantage of you', 'success in business means doing whatever it takes', 'there are no ethics in the real world...only survival of the fittest'. Teaching social responsibility in the eighties was tiring.

How much has this culture affected us all? It is very hard to remember a colleague suggesting a course of action on the grounds that it was morally right, rather than simply expedient. On the other hand, it is easy to remember instances of British politicians saying in interview that they had no view on the morality of various policies and could only comment on matters of efficiency. It might be argued that the end of consensus on moral questions in modern society means that it is no longer possible to talk of 'doing the right thing' and that the students comment's above reflect some obvious consequences of such a change.

If there is such a change and it is correct to speak of '...the end of ethics' as at least one writer has claimed (MacIntyre 1981), then any arguments in favour of ethical AI must be entirely parochial, but the arguments presented above show that being ethical is an expedient business strategy, in the long term.

At the same time it has to be said that there has been no shortage of attention, at least in print, to the social impacts of AI and related ethical issues. A small but significant group of people have been 'swimming against the tide': counselling caution in the headlong rush towards immediate profit from new and untried technologies. The BCS and ACM have consistently tried to remedy the lack of standards in the computing industry[1]. There have been some good books published in the ethical AI area[2] and many general AI books and conferences have included a section dedicated to these sorts of issues. Since 1987 there has even been a journal dealing primarily with the social impacts of AI[3].

The problem of changing the whatever it takes culture into one that takes more notice of ethical issues would seem to lie in providing the hook which might persuade those who regard themselves as hard-nosed to change their behaviour. One hook is provided by the long-term business advantages described above. Another might be to appeal to a sense of professional pride[4]. Perhaps the most important is the education of those who enter AI, and many other technologically-based professions. There are reasons to believe that this is both worthwhile and achievable. In fact, when some of the preceding observations are put together, AI seems to be in a position to gain a great deal from attention to ethical practices. There is not merely the benefits of appeal to wide markets that might apply to any technology, but some pointers to useful research goals. In order to improve its public acceptability AI can usefully distance itself from the image of direct human replacement.

Indeed many factors point towards ethical AI being widely practised in the future, one important reason is that all business will need to become more ethical. One area which cannot be ignored is environmental impact, for instance. 'Concern for the environment' is becoming a sine qua non of most forms of business activity. The change of attitude involved in expressing concern for the environment, even if not always genuine, will probably kill the whatever it takes view of business for ever. Businessmen are learning that they will be judged on rather more than short-term profits. This is probably the beginning of the sort of cultural change that may mark the end of the unthinking short-termism.

AI's environmental impacts are perhaps fairly small. However, this is not something to be ignored, but an important plus point for ethical AI. AI is a collection of research programs and technologies that does not threaten the environment and has possibilities for improving it. AI-controlled processes are, potentially at least, more efficient and reliable than processes controlled by older technologies. AI offers methods that enable human workers to escape dangerous environments. This sort of approach to 'selling' AI is likely to be more productive in the future than the continuation of previous approaches.

Similar observations could be made about presenting AI as a method of making computers more amenable to the general public. It has always been true, and often stated, that AI research goals such as natural language processing make computers more accessible to the user and take them away from the province of the technological elite. The same is true of knowledge-based (expert) systems. However, too much has been heard about such systems putting human experts out of work and far too little about the way in which they can make expert knowledge more accessible. To put this deficiency right would cost very little and would have considerable potential benefits in the era of ethical AI.

At the height of the Cold War funding was available for technologies that replaced human beings. There is no good reason to expect this to continue; in the foreseeable there is more chance of obtaining funding for technologies which instead develop human potential. There is little difficulty in recasting AI in this mould. An example is provided by the work of Perry Miller on critiquing systems (Miller 1986). The starting assumption of Miller's approach is that the user of a medical expert system should be treated as someone who has a great deal of professional knowledge and pride. This seems to be a more promising approach than the more conventional one of assuming that the user has no expertise and that the system can provide it all. For AI to continue to be of interest to funding organizations, this sort of approach should be given more stress than the use of AI to replace humans, expert or otherwise.

Signs of Change

At the time of writing it seemed worthwhile to conduct a small piece of telephone research. This suggested, at least the possibility that, an interesting process was taking place in the area of education in business ethics. There was no surprise at the London Business School, which cited lack of interest as a reason for not offering any business ethics component on their MBA courses. However, the Manchester Business School provided a surprise: it not only has an established commitment to the area, but is also currently engaged in setting up the 'International Centre for Corporate Responsibility'[5]. Imagine - a new institution dedicated solely to business ethics. This year has also seen the publication of an examination of the social, ethical, and environmental record of Britain's leading companies by an independent organization called New Consumer[6]. These are a couple of indications that there are ethics in the real world.

Of course, it takes more than these indications to persuade the majority of commercial leopards to change their spots. However there is an opportunity for change and AI has every reason to take advantage of it. As AI becomes so much harder to sell, the best selling point may be that it is ethically sound. Rebuilding the credibility of AI is a multi-faceted task, but an important first step must be to convince customers and funding authorities that the days of extravagant promises are over. It is, by now, obvious that there is a clear need for better and more generally applied standards throughout the computer industry. AI needs to be involved at the core of the move towards standards of good practice and towards the provision of more useful and reliable products.

A requirement for increased attention to the more general social effects of AI is also emerging in academia. A new generation of undergraduates needs to be well prepared for a world in which they cannot avoid taking responsibility for the wider consequences of their work. The defence that one is 'just a scientist' passed into history when Oppenheimer and his team created a new age as well as a new technology at Alamogordo in 1945. Tomorrow's scientists will be subject to much greater public scrutiny and criticism.

In addition, employers have the right to expect that graduates will be able to deal with greater public scrutiny and criticism. Wherever graduates in the new technologies choose to work they should be able to handle the ethical issues involved. Someone who claims to be 'merely a programmer' and needs constant supervision on ethical questions is not likely to be suitable for the sort of posts employers expect graduates to fill. It would seem, therefore, that some sort of basic grounding in the social and ethical responsibilities of scientists and technologists should be a required part of all first degree courses in science and technology.

Since there is a clear opportunity for all sorts of academic institutions to provide the necessary education and training in these areas, there may be some resurgence of academic interest. As has already been observed, there is no shortage of printed work. Perhaps, just perhaps, the 1990s will really be seen to be different from the 1980s in the degree of importance attached to the social and ethical consequences of AI. There will also be a need to encourage greater attention to ethical questions outside academia. Short courses for businessmen in computers and social responsibility: why not?

Notes

1. Both the ACM (Association of Computing Machinery) and the BCS (British Computer Society) have published codes of conduct for the guidance of their members (see references).

2. For example: Yazdani M. and Narayanan A. (1984) Council for Science and Society (1989) Erman D., Williams M., and Gutierrez C. (1990)

3. Gill K. (ed.), AI & Society, The Journal of Human and Machine Intelligence.

4. See for example Whitby B. (1988) .

5. The International Centre for Corporate Responsibility, Booth Street West, Manchester, M15 6PB.

6. Adams R., Caruthers J., and Hamil S. (1991).

References

Adams R., Caruthers J., and Hamil S. (1991). Changing Corporate Values, London, Kogan Page.

Association for Computing Machinery Bylaw 19, Code of Professional Conduct.

British Computer Society, Handbooks: Code of Conduct and Code of Practice, London, BCS Publications.

Council for Science and Society (1989). Benefits and Risks of Knowledge Based Systems, Oxford, OUP.

Erman D., Williams M., and Gutierrez C. (1990). Computers, Ethics and Society, Oxford, OUP.

Gill K.(ed), AI & Society, The Journal of Human and Machine Intelligence, London, Springer-Verlag .

MacIntyre A. (1981). After Virtue: a study in moral theory, Duckworth, London.

Miller, P.L. (1986). Expert Critiquing Systems, New York, Springer Verlag.

Whitby B. (1988). AI: A Handbook of Professionalism, Chichester, Ellis Horwood.

Yazdani M. and Narayanan A. (1984). AI: Human Effects, Chichester, Ellis Horwood.

The Computer Representation of Moral Reasoning

Introduction

'There is nothing either good or bad, but thinking makes it so'

Hamlet (Act 2 Scene 2)

In discussion of the building of computer-based advice systems there is a distinct tendency to assume, without obvious justification, that such systems are more suited to what are sometimes called the hard facts of human activity. That is to say that where a field involves vagueness, controversy, opinions, and difficult judgements it is automatically thought to be less suitable for representation on a computer than an area where the facts are thought naively to be clear-cut.

Thus expert systems have found acceptance in many engineering domains and have demonstrated potential, if nothing more, in the field of medical diagnosis. There is less enthusiasm for the development of expert systems to help in literary criticism or to advise in social skills, for example. The reasons for preferring 'hard' engineering and scientific type domains are many and complex. However, they undoubtedly include a prejudice that domains at the opposite extreme are extremely difficult, perhaps even impossible, to capture using contemporary techniques of computer representation.

In the area of computers and the law, this prejudice may contribute to the preference for research into the computer representation of highly-structured statute law such as the British Nationality Act 1981 (see, for example Sergot et al. 1986). Such research is undoubtedly useful. However, the use of AI in the legal area will be severely restricted if no consideration is given to the problems involved in the application of computer-based advice systems to areas which appear to be less highly-structured, such as case law. In order to be more generally useful, AI systems in law need to be able to handle the sorts of reasoning and knowledge involved in case law.

An additional argument in favour of research into the application of AI to some of the less highly structured domains involved in the law is provided by Marhalingham (Marhalingham 1991). She observes that even within statute law there are problems of computer representation of the type generally associated with case law. In particular, she asserts that case law does not readily afford uncontroversial rules suitable for the building of expert systems. To the extent that this observation is true of statute law in general, it will greatly reduce the possibility of building effective AI-based legal systems.

A further problem in the building of AI systems in law, which has sometimes been raised, is that, unlike their human counterparts, AI systems lack any representation of such general notions as justice and fairness. They are also entirely without understanding of human motivations. Thus they could not take into account the extent, for example, to which a plaintiff's anger or desire for revenge might influence his judgement about the relative strengths and weaknesses of his case.

These problems for the use of AI in law raise many philosophical issues that perhaps should receive consideration before proceeding to the implementation of AI systems. In terms of building working systems there seems to be two distinct possible courses of action. First, we could continue to build systems that deliberately do not attempt to incorporate any judgemental features and concentrate solely on those features of law (or other areas) that can unequivocally be rendered as logic (or whatever knowledge representation formalism we chose to use). Alternatively, we could experiment with attempts to capture elements of legal knowledge that are less formal in nature. There are prudential reasons for choosing the former course. For example, if we can be sure that only the more formal elements of a given area are covered by expert systems, we will know exactly where we stand with respect to the advice given by the expert system. It would contain absolutely no judgements, no intuitive elements, no concept of justice, and so on. Contemporary warnings about the limitations of expert systems would then apply. However, we are likely to choose the second course. There is already a good deal of work in this area. A moratorium on work in this area is not likely to prevent further research. This is because it is not possible in practice to exclude value judgements from the other sorts of knowledge that are incorporated into knowledge bases. Work in AI will stray into this area, however great is the intention to avoid it. This chapter describes an attempt to tackle one the most obvious, yet hardest, problems in this area, that of representing moral reasoning within a knowledge-based system. This includes a description of the design of a system that can carry out a form of debate on moral issues with its user. This is included, not so as to provide the technical directions, but to illustrate the successes and limitations of the approaches tried. It is suggested that these approaches could be incorporated into other types of knowledge-based systems, particularly expert systems in law that need to escape from the contemporary inability to handle concepts such as justice and fairness.

What is Moral Reasoning?

The problems of morality or ethics (the two terms are used interchangeably in this book) are central to human thinking. In our daily lives we must decide not only what can be done but also what ought to be done.

Not all decisions as to what ought to be done are moral decisions. A decision as to whether or not one 'ought' to make a particular move in a chess game, for example, is generally described by moral philosophers as involving a 'prudential ought', rather than a 'moral ought'. In AI terms this would be roughly equivalent to describing it as part of a search process for the optimum route to a given goal. In this example, the goal would be that of checkmating one's opponent and avoiding being checkmated by one's opponent, and what one 'ought', in this sense, to do describes that set of chess moves which are most likely to achieve this goal.

Giving an equally simple account of the meaning of 'ought' in the moral sense is undoubtedly too large and controversial a task for present purposes. It is accurate to describe the entire field of morality as still under vigorous, and often violent, debate. Nonetheless, a particular view of morality is implied by the approach described below and this needs to be explained in some detail.

When we consider what ought (in the moral sense) to be done, we carry out reasoning within a domain that has a number of special features. First of all, moral reasoning is essentially practical; that is to say that it must lead to a practical course of action in a given situation. Again, this is a controversial claim which will not be defended here. (For a competent defence, see Singer, 1979). Some other views of morality may seek to diminish or deny this feature and portray morality as describing a system of ideals which do not always apply in real-world situations, or as picking out the ideal rather than the most practical course of action. For present purposes, the notion of the ideal course of action is held to be interesting only in so far as it can guide practical action. There are also certain problems such as akrasia (backsliding) that highlight the difference between assenting to a moral principle and following it in practice, but these will be ignored. The crucial point is that moral reasoning is held to be, at least for present purposes, a form of reasoning that can and should guide action. This view of moral reasoning had important consequences in determining the final shape of the program.

Second, moral reasoning takes place within a domain that does not provide absolute right and wrong answers. Sometimes the domain may not afford clear answers of any sort. Again, this is ultimately a controversial claim, detailed discussion of which would be outside the scope of this book. More relevantly, to the extent that this claim is correct, it makes the domain of moral reasoning more difficult for conventional AI approaches to knowledge representation.

There is a dominance of logical or mathematical analyses at the basis of most of classical AI and a surprising amount of nouvelle AI knowledge representation. At a superficial level at least, this might suggest that a domain lacking a fundamental binary division into correct and incorrect would be difficult to represent.

In practice, the need to represent a domain without demanding that its contents be either true or false; right or wrong, does not pose any insuperable difficulties for current AI techniques. Nonetheless, it is worth remarking this feature of the domain of moral reasoning, since it is the attraction of applying AI techniques to novel and, perhaps, difficult domains that is part of the motivation for projects such as this.

Given a successful representation of the domain, there remains the problem of representing the type of reasoning conducted within it. It is assumed, for present purposes, that moral reasoning is not discontinuous from other forms of reasoning. This initial assumption was taken to entail that logic (of the ordinary, two-valued type) is applicable to moral reasoning. A further assumption has been made in this project that moral reasoning is essentially syllogistic; that is, roughly of the form: 'if p then q', 'p', 'therefore q'[1]. This assumption most certainly does not represent the claim that all moral reasoning has this form. However, the success of the program in simulating certain types of moral debate using syllogistic reasoning alone, represents a clear challenge to others to describe and model the other sorts of reasoning that might be involved in moral reasoning. These are briefly considered later in this chapter.

Some Existing AI Approaches to the Representation of Moral Reasoning

Although it might appear that the problem of how to represent moral reasoning in a knowledge-based system is a fairly obscure one, there have been a number of such attempts through the history of AI. An important early experiment in this domain was Abelson's Ideology Machine (Abelson 1973).

The Ideology Machine was not intended to simulate moral reasoning, but rather to model 'hot cognition'. This term relates to those factors of human reasoning that are strongly affectively influenced. Again, it is philosophically controversial as to whether moral reasoning is, and more importantly should be, strongly influenced by affect. For present purposes, a view of moral reasoning as almost completely free from affective influence is adopted. This view of moral reasoning is re-examined later.

The relevance of the Ideology Machine lies in its ability to handle knowledge of, and reasoning about, a domain that would, initially at least, appear to lie at the opposite end of a continuum from domains such as mathematics and logic that have received proportionately much more attention in AI research.

Another proposed program for this domain is described by Ennals (Ennals, 1986). This is a brief formalisation of some of the principles of Machiavelli's Il Principe in Prolog. Little more is essayed by Ennals than a demonstration that the rule-like presentation of Machiavelli's original work is eminently suitable for encoding in the form of Prolog clauses. However, this demonstration is another of the inspirations for the more detailed discussion of these issues that follows.

A more practical application of the representation of moral reasoning in an AI program actually in use is provided by the British Medical Association's (BMA) Consent to Medial Treatement (COMET) program (Sieghart, and Dawson, 1987). COMET is designed to be used by medical practitioners to assess the ethical implications of medical intervention.

COMET's design criteria reflected a very AI-like need to replace the sort of human interaction that represented a large proportion of telephone inquiries to the BMA ethics division (Private conversation with Dr. John Dawson). Despite this motivation, it functions merely as a computer-based checklist that ensures that the various ethical criteria for correct medical intervention have been met. It is, therefore, a relatively simple program (in AI terms) yet sufficiently effective in providing ethical advice to have been released to the medical profession in Britain.

The practical success of COMET suggests two further conclusions. First, programs involving some form of moral reasoning may well find practical applications. Second, a program is not required to achieve a high level of sophistication to be a worthwhile contribution to the state of the art in this area. This second point will not be explored further.

Some Remarks on Designing a Moral Reasoner: Why use GOFAI?

The use of more formal techniques of AI and the explicit representation of knowledge is so much out of fashion that more technically-minded readers will see it as somewhat strange that more contemporary techniques are not an obvious choice for this problem. There is set of very clear reasons why GOFAI (good old fashioned AI) is far more suitable for this area. First, there is the problem that nouvelle AI techniques are inscrutable. This was mentioned briefly in the final section of Chapter 2. It is exactly the sort of feature that is to be avoided in experiments in this area. A system that 'just performs' is undesirable because it may be mistakenly seen as having all manner of abilities that it does not in fact possess. It is far easier to see exactly what is lacking from a GOFAI system. This is important because a major part of the argument of this chapter is to contrast human moral reasoning with the sorts of reasoning that is undertaken by the systems considered in this chapter. An inscrutable system would be much more difficult to examine in this way. Second, as Boden (1995) has observed, GOFAI holds out better hope of understanding the nature of human decision making, particularly in areas like autonomy and creativity.

Among the features desired for a suitable representation of moral reasoning was its clear separation from the control aspects of the program. This would enable the use of a limited domain, or set of separate domains, of moral knowledge. It would also make it possible to inspect and alter the moral knowledge of the program, without having to run the program or interpret large portions of code.

The desirability of a separate knowledge base could have been met in several ways. Knowledge representations based upon concepts such as frames (Minsky 1974) or scripts (Schank and Abelson 1977), for example, would have satisfied this requirement. However, further useful features of a separate knowledge base are that it should be readable as English and contain no control information. This helped prompt the final choice of knowledge representation.

The knowledge base of the program is represented as 'if/then' rules, written so as to be readable in English. These are entirely separate and distinct from those parts of the program that interpret the rules and handle the control aspects of the program. A proportion of the rules are specific to the very small moral domains to which that particular knowledge base applies, but many are more general to the field of moral reasoning. Order of rules has no significance whatsoever.

Representing moral knowledge as 'if/then' rules has a number of consequences, not all felicitous for the objective of exploring moral reasoning. One felicitous consequence is that it can simplify (though perhaps deceptively so) the process of knowledge elicitation. That is to say that it is relatively easy to get humans to make moral statements that are in an 'if/then' format (particularly, it was discovered, if they are not required to assert them as universally true). These can then be incorporated into the system. A more complex representation would make the knowledge elicitation process more complex, inserting another stage between the human and knowledge base. Another of the more useful consequences is the fact that such a representation can be incorporated easily into a production system, and therefore techniques perfected in the field of expert systems are available to interpret and process the rules.

One of the disadvantages, on the other hand, of the use of 'if/then' rules is that it tends to prompt the use of syllogistic reasoning to draw conclusions from the knowledge base. It has already been observed that this is the only form of moral reasoning considered in this program and some of the consequences of this are developed in the section on the 'syllogistic constraint'. It should also be observed that it is very difficult to disagree with syllogistic reasoning. If people are presented with the rule 'if p then q', and the assertion 'p', they tend intuitively to agree with the conclusion 'q'. This feature enables the program, as actually developed, to carry the user along through deliberately controversial material. It should also be remarked that the effectiveness of this technique of reasoning may also be masking other defects of the program.

A second unfortunate feature of the use of 'if/then' rules, readable in English, is the way in which it encourages the implicit suggestion that this is in some way similar to the way in which humans represent moral rules. No conclusions, implicit or explicit, on the way in which humans represent moral knowledge or carry out moral reasoning lay behind this choice of representation.

Choosing a Limited Moral Domain

Since it would be unrealistic, if not impossible, to represent anything approaching the size of the average human's field of moral knowledge in one experimental program, further design decisions had to be made as to how best to limit the domain to be considered. An initial suggestion was made that a fairly limited subset of moral reasoning should be considered. An extremely limited and trivial subset could show principles that would apply to more general and more complex cases.

However, the problems involved in attempting to limit the domain of moral reasoning are more subtle than those involved in the circumscription of some other domains. In general, it can be said that attempts to limit moral reasoning are limitations on depth rather than scope. Given a specific moral problem, one can pursue questions as to what extent the problems raised are generalizable and what underlying principles need to be examined, asserted or retracted. Let us call the dimension of moral reasoning along which this pursuit takes place the depth of moral reasoning. On the other hand, given a specific moral principle, one can pursue questions as to what range of practical cases require decisions to be based upon this principle. Let us call the dimension of this pursuit the scope of moral reasoning.

A good example of a deliberate decision to limit the depth of moral (political, if you prefer) reasoning is provided by Abelson's Ideology Machine. This contained a number of basic principles embodied in what Abelson called a 'master script'. This included such basic principles as: 'the communists want to dominate the world' and that 'the communists are continually using schemes to try and bring about world domination'. These basic principles, encoded in the master script, were not open to any sort of modification while the program was running (Abelson 1973). The program was not intended to examine the consequences of believing or not believing in such basic principles; it was a model of someone who believed such things without question.

It was considered undesirable to limit the depth of the domain in this way, since that would nullify the special features of interest about the domain mentioned above. What was required, therefore, was a method of limiting the scope, but not the depth, of the domain.

Two methods of limiting the scope of the domain under consideration were employed in the final version of the program. The first was to consider a single issue, in this case abortion, and the second was to present the user with a scenario requiring a difficult moral choice. The advantages of the first method were chiefly that the program could be said to conduct a form of moral debate on an issue that was practically relevant and to which there was (for design purposes at least) no simple absolute answer. The form of debate was therefore as open-ended as could reasonably be achieved. An important guiding principle was therefore that the rule base should both contain and facilitate examination of the most basic principles involved in this area.

The second method of limitation of domain was to describe a scenario requiring some action that would imply a moral decision. In this case the decision was loosely based upon a situation from Harper Lee's To Kill a Mockingbird. The user must take a decision and this decision is taken to imply the adoption of a position with respect to certain moral questions about guilt, innocence and killing.

The Critiquing System

Having adopted a form of representation for the moral domains to be used by the program that closely resembles a production system, it would be natural to employ fairly conventional expert system technology to perform computation using the knowledge represented about those domains. However, a conventional expert system would not necessarily be applicable for the domain of moral reasoning. A classical expert system would typically use a body of production rules similar to those chosen for this program to analyse a user- supplied problem and suggest an answer to that problem. In some areas, such as medical diagnosis, this approach can be satisfactory, however it is not suitable for an area where there is held to be no particular right answer.

Suppose that a moral reasoner were built according to this approach. The user would supply a moral problem and the system would eventually respond with something like: 'the morally correct course of action under the circumstances is...'. Such a system would be of limited usefulness. This sort of interaction takes place between human beings only when one of them is deemed to have some sort of moral authority. If the domain of moral reasoning has the features outlined above, it would be highly undesirable for humans to feel that any system could meaningfully provide this sort of response. It is important to remember that if there is no single right answer a state of continuous debate may be more useful and realistic than agreement. Furthermore, it has been argued that there may be dangerous consequences of attributing any sort of moral authority to AI systems (Whitby 1988). The next chapter, Implications of the Computer Representation of Moral Reasoning, also explores some of these issues.

Even if a system were felt to be acceptable on these grounds, it would encounter difficulties over the assumption, mentioned above, that the domain is such as not to yield correct and incorrect answers. The classical expert system approach might attempt to deal with this by the use of certainty factors. In what is perhaps the classical expert system, MYCIN (Shortliffe 1976), all the production rules have certainty factors attached and the conclusion reached by the system, a medical diagnosis, is also given a certainty factor calculated from the certainty factors of the rules that were fired during the operation of the system. It would not make sense, in knowledge representation terms, to attach certainty factors to the sort of rules used for this program. There is no obvious measure of probability that represents the degree to which we can conclude that, for example: 'if all moral issues are a matter of individual judgement, then there is no overall moral principle that applies'. This rule simply is or is not the case. The syllogistic force of this rule would be invalidated by making it in some sense probabilistic; and the certainty factor attached would be both meaningless and arbitrary. Another approach to the lack of absolute right and wrong in this domain was thought to be better.

The approach adopted was inspired by the work of Perry Miller (Miller 1984, 1986) in developing 'critiquing expert systems'. A critiquing system does not adopt the classical approach described above: in the field of medical diagnosis, Miller suggests that traditional expert systems have been designed to simulate human experts. A critiquing system, by contrast, assumes that the human user has already formed a diagnosis or a plan for patient mangement. The system then provides a critique of that plan, discussing the pros and cons with the user. Miller identifies a number of advantages of the critiquing approach in the area of medical diagnosis. These include the physician having to think through the problem for himself and that medical practice must allow for idiosyncratic variations. Under this last claim, Miller also suggests that:

'There are frequently several ways to approach a particular problem, and it is seldom that one approach is 'right' and the others are 'wrong'.' (Miller, 1984, p3).

This approach seemed ideally suited to the domain of moral reasoning. Not only does it avoid the obvious absurdity and irrelevance of the sort of moral reasoning system that simply gave pronouncements as described above, but it also offers a technique to deal with the problem of there being no one correct solution to problems within the moral domain.

The system, as built, is not a critiquing system in Miller's sense. It does not gather facts from the user and use these to prepare a critique of the user's plan in exactly the way that Miller envisages. Although this would be a perfectly reasonable way to handle moral reasoning and the program could have been arranged to do this, the program is rendered more interesting to use by making it more interactive. Thus the user is presented with the implications of his choice immediately after making it and asked to make a further choice.

There is another significant difference between this system and Miller's model of a critiquing system. This lies in the way in which the moral reasoner obtains a goal at the outset and reasons back from that goal rather than towards it as might be the case with medical diagnosis.

Knowledge Elicitation Issues

Were the program considered to be a conventional expert system, then great emphasis would presumably be placed on knowledge engineering. It would certainly seem that the sort of sensitive, controversial material contained in the two rule bases would have to be gathered most carefully and checked for accuracy. Indeed, the rule bases were originally envisaged as smaller and perhaps reflecting some sort of moral truth.

This view of the knowledge elicitation issues involved turned out to be almost totally false. The program as developed was found to benefit from as large a number of rules as possible. More surprisingly, it was found that the content of the rules was far less significant than had been imagined. As long as the rules met syntactic constraints, primarily that they could be chained with other rules and used in the syllogistic reasoning process, their content was relatively unimportant.

These properties are easily explained by the features forced upon the program by the design decisions discussed in the last section. The effect of presenting all relevant antecedents and consequents to the user for agreement or disagreement is that the content is relatively unimportant as far as the program is concerned. Judgements about the semantic content of rules are made primarily by the user. The program is more concerned with the syntax of the rules. That is to say the way in which they fit into the chain of syllogisms that forms the structure of the debate.

Nonetheless, a certain amount of conventional knowledge elicitation was implicit in the construction of the rule bases, and this is an area where further attention might be worthwhile. Informal tests of the program revealed that users were often unhappy with what might be called the 'quantification' of many of the rules - for example: 'usually morally wrong', 'can choose', 'ought to choose', and so on. Of course, sensible rules in this domain must involve such 'quantification', but it is perhaps semantically laden. This point will be taken up again in the conclusions.

The User Interface

At the outset it was decided to produce the simplest possible user interface so as to concentrate on knowledge representation issues. This led to the employment of menu-selection techniques. The user is presented with a limited field of possible responses and asked to select only one. At the outset of interaction with the program, this requirement to select only one option is fortuitous in that the user can be trapped into a single stance with respect to the issue under discussion. This facilitates a debate on the issue.

As the debate continues, the user is presented with a menu that allows agreement or disagreement with the notion (that is, the moral claim) under discussion or permits the user to query why this particular notion is being presented by the program. If the user asks why the particular notion under discussion is being presented, a justification is presented in terms of the relevant rule and the portion of the syllogism to which the user has already assented. This may, in practice, be either the antecedent or consequent of the relevant rule, depending on the direction in which the rule base is being searched.

Some Conclusions

Many deep and difficult philosophical problems are associated with the attempt to represent moral reasoning within a computer program. Perhaps the primary question is whether, and to what extent, moral reasoning differs from other sorts of reasoning. One extreme view would be that moral reasoning is identical with other forms of reasoning and merely conducted in a different domain. If this were the case then we would expect little problem in designing and building advice-giving systems in the moral domain. Such systems need be no different from those that advise on geological features or medical diagnosis. At the other extreme are views that describe human moral reasoning as based on intuition or divine inspiration. On these views, any computer representation can be nothing more than the most grotesque of caricatures.

A further question is whether and to what extent moral reasoning is essentially logical. However, in debate and perhaps in all forms of discussion, logic is generally more persuasive than other methods of reasoning. We tend to give more weight to a logically correct argument than one which seems intuitively correct, though there may be an unresolved tension, particularly for people who feel strongly about their intuitions.

No attempt has been made to describe this investigation into moral reasoning as an example of cognitive modelling. No conclusions are drawn as to how humans conduct moral reasoning. However, it is inevitable that much of the work of this project will be incorrectly seen as part of a piece of cognitive modelling. Many comparisons have been drawn between the behaviour of the program and the behaviour of humans under certain conditions. With the possible exception of the Almighty, it seems probable that only humans conduct moral reasoning. Thus any attempt to analyse it, however motivated, cannot escape such comparisons.

It is very difficult to deliberately and directly compare the program with human moral reasoning. Not only do we lack the sort of psychological research which might facilitate this, but once again the area is philosophically controversial. If moral intuitions are taken as an essentially unanalysable component of human moral reasoning, then this sort of attempt to use cognitive modelling techniques must fail to capture this component. Similar remarks would apply to the view that moral reasoning is directly or indirectly influenced by an individual's relationship to God.

This is not the place to comment on these philosophical and psychological problems. They are explored more fully in the next two chapters. Recognition of them, though, must entail that any comparison of the methods and representations of the program with those of humans must be made with the utmost caution. Taking full account of this, there are specific deficiencies in the program which, it might be argued, provide sharp contrast between what it does and what humans might be said to do when they carry out moral reasoning. The most important of these are discussed in the following sections.

The Syllogistic Constraint

The concentration on syllogistic reasoning alone is a limitation of the program which is highly important in suggesting future work in this area. It has already been observed that the concentration on the syllogism in this project should not suggest that this is the only form of reasoning employed in the moral domain. However, any other form of reasoning would be of use only to the extent that its technique was accepted by users and of interest only to the extent that the reasoning techniques employed could inform user's own reasoning about the problem. No reasoning technique other than the syllogism meets these criteria so well. The reasoning techniques implicit in the program have considerable intuitive appeal.

It would have been interesting to explore other techniques of reasoning as part of the project. These would not have been more sophisticated logical techniques, but rather inductive techniques of reasoning.

Given the intuitive appeal of the syllogism, moral debate tends not to focus on the 'if p then q, p, therefore q' stage of moral reasoning. It is more likely to focus on whether or not the precise problem under discussion is indeed an instance of 'p'. For example, protagonists of differing views of abortion are quite likely to agree that if an action involves killing innocent people then it is morally wrong. They are more likely to disagree over whether or not abortion is an action which involves killing innocent people.

This aspect of moral debate perhaps deserves to recieve more attention. The question of whether a given example is indeed an instance of 'p' is a familiar AI problem. It has close connections to problems in vision and natural language processing. Some of the techniques currently being developed in those areas, such as neural nets, may have something to offer in this area.

The Semantic Deficit

The program, at present, contains no representation of the semantics of moral reasoning. When the rules are read as English by a human reader the antecedents and consequents can be assumed to have semantic content. The only account taken by the program of these antecedents and consequents is the performance of pattern-matching operations with them. The program interprets the antecedents and consequents simply as Prolog atoms and can merely detect when two are identical. The suggestion that 'mass murder is sometimes morally justified', may fill the human user with horror, but the program has no representation of the content of this clause. The clause has simply been output by the program because it has been recognised as part of the 'mass murder rule' in the rule base.

Some commentators might see this semantic deficit as rendering the entire experiment described in this chapter pointless. They might say that it is human understanding of the semantic content of moral rules and language that forms the basis of moral reasoning.

Such a simple deduction from the semantic deficit cannot be permitted, however. There is still much work to be done in this area, but the semantic deficit of this program certainly does not render it entirely pointless. It indicates an area that needs serious philosophical consideration.

One important question that is raised by this experiment is the degree to which something like moral reasoning can be modelled without paying any attention to its semantic content. The fact that the program achieves a certain level of performance without the sort of semantic knowledge which, it might be claimed, humans have, can raise questions as to how important the semantic content of moral reasoning is for humans.

Consider a human teacher of moral reasoning. She might put a moral problem to her class, much in the way the program does. An individual pupil might react to this problem very strongly because it is associated with her own painful memories and regrets. The teacher may or may not pick up this reaction, however; even if she does, it is not appropriate for her to take account of it in directing the course of the discussion. The discussion must be shaped by the underlying logic.

It is in this area that extensions to the project have been proposed. The use of a frame-based representation to add this sort of semantic content to the rules will add an interesting dimension to the sort of moral reasoning possible. Of course, this still leaves out of consideration several factors that might be considered essential to human moral reasoning. In particular, there is the problem, mentioned above, of the lack of any affective content to the types of reasoning considered.

Other Potential Applications of the Techniques Involved

Although the attempt to understand and reproduce moral reasoning is unlikely to become a mainstream area of AI research, many of the features of the domain discussed and the techniques used have possible applications in other areas of AI research. Some other domains have a number of interesting similarities to that of moral reasoning. The sort of system described in this chapter could possibly be applied in medical diagnosis and, with an improved user interface, as the basis for an Intelligent Teaching System.

Perhaps the most obvious application of the techniques examined in moral reasoning is in the design of Legal Advice Systems. In this area there is a similar need to find representations that do not automatically imply the existence of absolute right or wrong answers. The domain of the law can be seen as a body of absolute knowledge, but there are many objections to such a view (Leith, 1986) and it could be seen as more like the domain of moral reasoning. If the law is viewed instead as a domain in which there can and should be disagreement, then the approach employed by this project and the use of critiquing systems such as this would seem to be a useful development.

Notes

1. This is not, strictly speaking, equivalent to the Aristotelian syllogism. It is closer to the medieval modus ponens with the addition of the usual inclusion of a 'universal affirmative' ("everything which has F has G"). Since the reasoning is actually encoded in Prolog, which is formally a subset of predicate calculus, it would be more accurate to claim that it has been assumed that all moral reasoning can be captured by predicate calculus. However, all that is needed for the purposes of this chapter is the use (or perhaps misuse) of the adjective 'syllogistic' to capture the very limited approach to reasoning taken in this project. It is to be hoped that readers with classical and logical knowledge will tolerate this inexactitude.

References

Abelson, R.P. (1973) 'The Structure of Belief Systems' in Schank, R.C and Colby, K.M. (eds) Computer Models of Thought and Language, San Francisco, Freeman.

Boden, M. (1995) 'Artificial Intelligence and Human Dignity' in Cornwell, J. (ed) Nature's Imagination, The Frontiers of Scientific Vision, Oxford University Press. Ennals, R. (1986), Star Wars: A question of initiative, Chichester, John Wiley & Sons pp.219-219.

Ennals, R. (1986) Star Wars: A question of Initiative, Chichester, John Wiley.

Leith, P (1986) Fundamental Errors in Legal Logic Programming, The Computer Journal, Vol 29, no 6 1986.

Mahalingham, I (1991) 'Computers in Law – Hard Cases' in Narayanan and Bennun (eds) 1991) Law, Computer Science and Artificial Intelligence, New Jersey, Ablex.

Miller, P.L. (1984) A Critiquing Approach to Expert Computer Advice: Attending, Boston Ma.. Pitman.

Miller, P.L. (1986) Expert Critiquing Systems, New York, Springer- Verlag.

Minsky, M. (1974) A Framework for Representing Knowledge, M.I.T. AI Lab Memo No 306.

Schank, R.C. and Abelson, R.P. (1977), Scripts, plans goals and understanding, New Jersey, Lawrence Erlbaum.

Seighart, P. and Dawson, J., (1987), Computer -aided medical ethics in Journal of Medical Ethics, 13 pp.185-188.

Sergot, M.J., Sadri, F., Kowalski, R.A., Kriwaczek, F. Hammond, P. and Cory, H.T. (1986) The British Nationality Act as a logic program, Communication of the ACM 29 (5), pp370-386.

Shortliffe, E.H. (1976), Computer-Based Medical Consultations: MYCIN, New York, Elsevier.

Singer, P. (1979) Practical Ethics, Cambridge University Press.

Whitby, B. (1988) Artificial Intelligence: A Handbook of Professionalism, Chichester, Ellis Horwood.

Implications of the Computer Representation of Moral Reasoning

Introduction

The possibility of AI-based systems giving moral advice or training may seem a remote future possibility. In fact, it is no such thing. One of the the most important reasons for including this chapter is the fact that such systems, or systems purporting to do this, are already in use.

This is clearly something that deserves extensive examination. There are complex and difficult questions raised by the possibility of taking moral advice from a machine. These questions become even more complex and difficult when one continues to consider the related, but only slightly more remote, possibilities of a machine generating new moral knowledge or taking moral decisions autonomously (these possibilities are collectively referred to in this book as 'moral reasoning'). This chapter is an attempt to open debate on what seems to be an important set of philosophical problems.

Some of the technical problems and possibilities of actually building such a system have been discussed elsewhere in the last chapter. For present purposes it is largely necessary to ignore the technical issues and to take strenuous efforts to avoid being distracted into discussion of what is and is not technically possible. The questions with which this chapter is concerned are those of the rights and wrongs of building and using such systems. Readers who need more information about what sort of techniques might be involved in building such a system should consult the previous chapter ('The Computer Representation of Moral Reasoning').

Among the questions that need to be addressed are why such systems are likely to be developed and whether or not we should have moral doubts about the building of such systems. These are not primarily technical questions.

Why build such a system?

There are many reasons why AI and associated technologies are likely to become involved in the area of moral reasoning. In fact, there are so many reasons that one would be foolish to claim anything like an exhaustive list. Perhaps the most obvious reason is simply to determine whether or not it can be done. However, this sort of pure curiosity is unlikely to provide the basis for the funding of an extended research program.

A better candidate for funding might be the progressive extension of various types of advice-giving systems into the moral area. For example, a system designed to give decision support for investment management might include in its knowledge base a certain amount on ethical matters. This might include representation of the legislation affecting investment, basic business ethics, representation of what is meant by 'ethical investment', and so on. The designers of this system might have no intention of becoming involved in the ethical area, but during the building of the system find, first, that advice has to be given on such matters, and second, that the human experts involved frequently talk of such matters as affecting their decisions.

A similar gradual inclusion of moral knowledge is likely to occur in the development of legal and medial advice systems. The relationship between the law and morality is complex and controversial, but systems that simply encode legislation without regard for the moral assumptions that permeate a given society may well turn out to be too limited in practice. A similar sort of observation applies to medical expert systems. There are many ethical questions involved in the practice of medicine and there is little point in building a system that takes no account of this. If a system advises a doctor to perform a diagnostic test that would be unethical under the given circumstances then its advice is worthless (or so we must hope). Similarly, if the system concludes by suggesting an unethical treatment we should regard it as useless in practice.

Most AI researchers would regard these requirements of advice-giving systems as obvious and fairly unproblematical. However, there are difficulties in not deliberately making explicit the inclusion of ethical knowledge into such a system. It is an established design principle of knowledge-based systems that various types of knowledge should be represented as separately and explicitly as possible. To simply modify a medical advice system to ensure that it always gives ethical advice, without making explicit the specifically ethical nature of such advice could lead to inconsistencies elsewhere in the system. Good knowledge engineering practice would be to represent medical knowledge in a set of rules[1] and to represent ethical knowledge in a separate set of rules within the rule base. This principle might well be thought worth extending further to the 'human interface' part of the system. In other words, when the system delivers advice as output it should indicate to the user whether or not ethical knowledge was involved in generating that particular piece of advice.

By following uncontroversial and commonplace design principles for building an advice-giving system, therefore, we find it desirable to both include ethical knowledge and to make it explicit. This in turn will raise interesting questions about knowledge elicitation - how we obtain the relevant knowledge from human experts so that it may be encoded within the system. If we restrict such systems to areas where the ethical issues are fairly uncontroversial, progress may be possible. In areas (and there are many) where the ethical issues are not generally agreed, there seems no clear way to proceed. One option discussed elsewhere in this book ('The Computer Representation of Moral Reasoning') is to set up the system to enter into discussion and debate with the user. A more common practice is simply to print a message that the area involves controversy and that the user should discuss the matter with colleagues if he or she is unsure.

Neither of these approaches is entirely satisfactory. They both entail that the system will fail to achieve its primary design objective of producing advice as output. If a user requires advice, he or she is unlikely to be interested in discussion or being referred elsewhere. For this sort of reason there will always be a very strong temptation for system designers to ignore the problems and set up the system to produce fairly definite conclusions. As a technical aside, it is worth noting that, if the system contains a rich representation of moral knowledge, it will therefore be able to generate plausible explanations of its conclusions, however definite and arbitrary.

In conclusion, therefore, AI-based moral advisors are likely to be built primarily because work on other types of advice-giving systems is likely to gradually expand into this area. The already widespread use of AI-based systems to give advice in various fields will gradually expand to include ethical elements. This suggests a relatively unexamined process whereby mainly technical developments slowly, perhaps imperceptibly, become ethically significant. In order to be able to form some conclusions about whether this development is desirable or undesirable, it is first necessary to look in greater detail at the status of the knowledge used by such systems.

'Genuine' or 'Artificial' Moral Knowledge?

Having examined some reasons why systems that give advice are likely to include moral elements, some difficult questions are raised about the status of the moral knowledge contained within these systems. Many people will find it difficult to accept that the sort of information that could conceivably be encoded in electronic form could also have the same status as their own moral beliefs. There are many reasons for asserting that the type of moral knowledge held by AI-based systems is fundamentally different from that held by human beings. This section will attempt to examine as many of those reasons as possible.

First, there are various objections to the status of computer-based moral reasoning that are based on ignorance of the technology. These might include claims that computers can only do what their programmers tell them to do, or that they can only proceed in a deductive fashion from premises to conclusion. Both these claims are false. Readers who doubt their falsehood should consult a writer who deals in detail with these issues (Boden 1987) or an AI introductory text (Charniak and McDermott 1985). It is important to be clear at the outset of this discussion that we are discussing systems that can reason with uncertain information, take guesses, use approximations and similar techniques, and (on occasion) produce genuinely novel results. This is true of existing AI technology and not any form of speculation about the future.

Despite these capabilities, some writers have refused to accept that AI and its associated technologies work upon and produce 'genuine' knowledge (for example Searle 1984 and Penrose 1989). Moral knowledge is obviously a special case, but almost certainly one for which these writers would assert that it is merely a repository for essentially human knowledge. In this respect they might claim that an AI system, no matter how sophisticated, 'contains knowledge' only in the sense that other non-human repositories of knowledge do, like books, for example.

One might wryly observe at this point that humans have, perhaps, attributed too much status to non-human repositories of moral knowledge throughout history. However, there are crucial differences between AI systems and, for example, books. The most important is that it is not usually claimed that books can generate new knowledge, in the sense that the claim is made about AI systems. It might be argued that books can prompt their readers to look at familiar material in a novel way that in turn can cause them to draw fresh conclusions. This is subtly, but importantly, different from the way in which AI systems might be claimed to operate - reassembling knowledge, independent of human beings, so as to produce new conclusions.

This is a claim that can justifiably be made for at least one AI system - Lenat's Automatic Mathematician (AM) (Lenat 1977, 1983). This system was designed to explore mathematical concepts according to how 'interesting' it considered them. Not only did AM produce many arithmetical concepts and theories, it occasionally discovered new routes to them including some that prompted human mathematicians to develop shorter proofs. If moral knowledge is relevantly similar to mathematical knowledge, there is at least the theoretical possibility that some future 'Automatic Moralist' may prompt human experts to revise their moral codes.

Of course, the expression 'relevantly similar' in the last sentence requires detailed philosophical examination. Many people feel that moral knowledge is fundamentally different from mathematical knowledge, however this feeling does not always reflect serious consideration; it may well reflect a desire to avoid serious consideration. The remainder of this chapter is, primarily, an initial attempt at such consideration.

It would be most convenient at this stage to fall back upon pre-AI prejudices and say that such a system could only reflect the moral knowledge of its designers. This option, unfortunately, is not open to us. An example has been given of one system that is more accurately described as producing new knowledge than as merely regurgitating existing knowledge. If programs can accurately be described as creating new knowledge then there is no reason, in principle, why a system working with moral rather than mathematical knowledge could not create new, that is, previously unknown, knowledge in the moral domain. The question with which we are concerned here is whether AI-generated new knowledge about the moral domain should be considered to be genuine or artificial moral knowledge.

This distinction would be absurd if applied to the mathematical domain. It would be very difficult to argue that any knowledge about the mathematical domain was not mathematical knowledge. Provided it met the usually agreed standards of consistency, it would make no difference whether its point of origin was human, artificial, or some combination of both. This is precisely what has happened in the case of AM.

One important difference between the two domains stems from the fact that implications about the way human beings should respond to AI-generated moral propositions are more obscure but, nevertheless, much more important than any implications about how human beings should respond to AI-generated mathematical propositions. This difference is most certainly not irrelevant and may well be a major motivation for far greater concern about the use of AI systems in the moral area than in the mathematical area. On the other hand, our concern about the far greater social implications of an 'Automatic Moralist' rather than those of an Automatic Mathematician is, strictly speaking, irrelevant to the central question of whether or not we are dealing with 'genuine' moral knowledge. This question would seem to depend on, among other things, the extent to which moral knowledge and reasoning is similar to mathematical knowledge and reasoning.

Granted the abilities of the technology, some might object that moral knowledge or reasoning involves a number of other elements that cannot be captured in present or reasonably foreseeable technology. One candidate for such an element might be the ability to empathize. Much moral reasoning has been held to involve the principle of 'universalisation'. In terms of formal moral reasoning this involves the stipulation that a moral principle should be applicable in all relevantly similar circumstances (Hare 1963). In commonsense and non-formal circumstances it is sometimes rendered as: 'How would you feel if you were in that position?' or 'How would you feel if someone did that to you?'. This in turn has been related to the psychological ability to put oneself in the position of another individual (Wright 1971). It seems reasonable to observe, to the extent that human moral reasoning depends on the ability to put oneself in the position of another, that AI-based systems are going to be unable to perform anything more than a crude simulation of this sort of reasoning.

The position is considerably more complex than this, however. It is certainly not obvious that the ability to empathize is always required of humans. Sometimes we may prefer our moral judgements to be impartial. If we were to extend the need to empathize to its ultimate conclusion then we might feel that there was a problem in male gynaecologists making ethical judgements about their patients or celibate priests making moral judgements about certain sexual matters. When we make moral judgements about the treatment of animals, the ability to empathize may be a disadvantage since we will often tend to project human wants and needs on to very different creatures and perhaps make inappropriate moral judgements as a result.

However, there is clearly a greater problem in the case of the AI system that not only cannot empathize on a particular issue, but makes no pretence to empathize at all. The question that needs to be answered in this case is: can genuine (as opposed to simulated or synthetic) moral reasoning be undertaken by a system that does not share human experience or emotions? This is a question that has not often been directly addressed by philosophers, but has a close relation to more familiar philosphical questions.

The most prominent of these familiar philosophical questions is that of whether morality can be, at a basic level, construed as rational. This question has been repeatedly addressed in various contexts by moral philosophers. An interesting, contemporary discussion of this question is undertaken by Danielson (Danielson 1992). Danielson proposes the use of computer-simulated moral agents to explore what sort of moral interactions can take place between them. In this case, the constraints placed upon the simulated agents allow examination of the consequences of various interactions between them. His ultimate philosophical goal is to demonstrate by this methodology that morality follows logically from rational self-interest.

Danielson's project raises many issues that are orthogonal to the theme of this chapter but, to the extent to which it is successful, provides a strong argument that morality, construed as founded upon rational self-interest, can be represented within and manipulated by computer systems. If we conclude that morality is some sort of logical consequence of rational self-interest by independent, but interacting, agents then the sort of objections so far discussed do not apply. Having appropriate emotions or an ability to empathize or the would then be simply irrelevant to the ability to perform moral reasoning.

Danielson starts from a position of claiming that morality is fundamentally rational, but many philosophers have made contrary claims. These philosophers might have a further reason for doubting that some sort of AI system could carry out genuine moral reasoning: namely its lack of any 'moral sense' or 'conscience' (where 'conscience' is understood as something other than the internalization of external moral code). If one sees moral behaviour, and even any judgement as to whether behaviour is moral, as stemming from some sort of non-cognitive human 'moral sense' (of which intuition would be a plausible example), then the AI system is at a great disadvantage. This would be one reason for claiming that the sort of moral knowledge embodied in systems such as that described in the previous chapter is not genuine moral knowledge.

In order to believe that humans have a moral sense of this sort, it is not necessary to subscribe to the view of moral philosophy known as 'intuitionism'. However, if one believes that the authority of morality ultimately derives from some sort of moral intuition possessed by normal human beings, then an artificial system may be unable to 'perceive' moral truths in the relevant sense. This does not, in principle, rule out the possibility of endowing an AI system with a similar sort of moral sense, but adherents of this sort of view are unlikely to give much consideration to this possibility.

Many philosophers have argued for the primacy of moral intuitions (Prichard 1949, Ross 1930). The view (usually called intuitionism) that human beings have a set of moral intuitions that shape their moral judgements is often also taken to imply that any logical or philosophical analysis is merely an ex-post formalisation of those intuitions. If this is the case, then knowledge-based advisors on moral issues might be argued to be absurd. It would be far more appropriate for humans to trust their moral intuitions than to rely on any sort of representation of a formalisation of those intuitions. Since any AI-based advice-giving system would lack intuitions it would once again be seen as, at best, a caricature of human moral reasoning.

We must expect a similar position from those who relate moral reasoning to some spiritual aspect of humanity. If moral codes stem ultimately from God or form part of the relationship between humanity and God, then artifacts, no matter how ingeniously constructed, cannot enter into this relationship. If 'conscience' (in its non-cognitive sense) is described as a product of human spiritual or religious capabilities, then this would completely invalidate the possibility of including any moral sense in an AI system.

A more often stated limitation of AI systems is their complete lack of 'common sense' - a difficult concept to unpack. As a first approximation we could say that the moral knowledge contained within an AI system would not contain any realistic representation of the experience of living as a human being in human society. This is undoubtedly true and likely to remain true for the forseeable future. It is not clear how we could include such a nebulous and ill-defined item into the knowledge base of an AI system. Of course, a major problem with ill-defined concepts is that it is hard to base important arguments upon them. The only way that a proponent of this objection could claim that the lack of common sense actually mattered would be if it somehow caused defective performance in the AI system. This would be difficult to establish without begging the question at issue.

In other words, if AI-based moral advisors tended to generate different answers from humans they would simply be modified to make their answers more acceptable. In the same way that medical and financial expert systems have been developed to give perfectly acceptable diagnoses and advice without the benefit of common sense, so moral advisors will be developed without it. The lack of common sense will only matter if it makes the whole project impossible. That is, if common sense is required to make moral judgements in a way in which it is not required for medical or financial judgements. It is precisely this question of what exactly is required of a moral judgement that is at issue here.

Mention of the problem of including nebulous and ill-defined concepts into a knowledge-base will have perhaps prompted more technically-minded readers to consider the possibility of using a connectionist[2] approach to this problem. This is not an attractive option for two reasons. First, to train a neural net to incorporate human experience in this general sense would present insuperable practical problems. In the end the only satisfactory approach might turn out to be to somehow give the net all, or at least a very large proportion, of the experiences that a human being receives. To attempt to short-circuit this process by training the net on some distillation from human experience (perhaps a large number of poetic and literary accounts of the human experience relevant to the formation of moral judgements) moves the project back towards conventional knowledge engineering. If we are prepared to distil human experience in this way, why not simply encode human moral expertise in the way in which we encode human medical or financial expertise?

Second, and far more importantly, the inscrutable nature of neural nets makes them unsuitable for application in areas such as moral reasoning. Even if we could train a neural net to give satisfactory answers to an interesting range of moral questions, there would be no way to ask it to justify its conclusions. Unlike more conventional approaches to knowledge representation, the internal structure of the net need not correspond to any previously determined external structure in the knowledge being represented. Asking the system to justify its conclusions is therefore likely to be pointless. Enthusiasts for the connectionist approach might feel with some justification that this is analogous to frequent human responses in this area. We should not be surprised to hear someone say something along the lines of: 'I just feel that it's wrong, I can't say why', for example. Nevertheless, no matter how interesting the ability to build AI systems that produce human-like responses may be, it is not a promising avenue to pursue in designing advice-giving systems. Recall for a moment the reasons discussed above for the likely construction of AI-based moral advisors. These systems will need to be adept at justifying and explaining the reasoning processes that have lead to a particular conclusion, just as present-day advice-giving systems in fields such as medicine and engineering are. For this reason, connectionism will most probably not be the favoured approach in the computer representation of moral reasoning.

Ultimately, the decision as to whether or not a system (built under the limitations of contemporary technology) is carrying out genuine moral reasoning depends more on our views on the nature of morality than on any technical matter. It has always been a matter of debate in moral philosophy as to whether knowing, rather than feeling, on the relevant issues is at the centre of moral judgements. The introduction of AI systems does little more than provide a focus for this familiar debate.

However, this focus may itself provide a strong argument in favour of cautious experimentation in this area. AI work may provide some relevant experimental data as to the degree to which purely logical or purely 'knowing' systems can perform the same sort of moral reasoning as human beings. If it were to turn out that the present thrust of research, which pays little or no attention to emotion or intuition, could produce systems which made acceptable moral judgements, then this would suggest that human emotion or intuition was not vital to human moral judgement. The use, as opposed to the development, of systems that generate moral advice could then be seen as a project similar to Danielson's - a technologically-based inquiry into the nature of morality itself.

The Case For the Building of AI-based Moral Reasoners

In spite of certain problems and dangers there are a number of arguments in favour of developing AI-based moral reasoners. One of the most important is that there exist 'knowledge deficits'. That is to say that many real world problems stem from the lack of knowledge, or to be more precise, the right sort of information not being available at the right place and at the right time. Many problems stem from the lack of moral knowledge in particular. These problems can sometimes be countered by the introduction of computer-based systems. An example of such a knowledge deficit is provided by one of the systems already in use - The British Medical Association (BMA)'s COMET program (Sieghart, and Dawson, 1987). COMET, designed to be used by medical practitioners to assess the ethical implications of medical intervention, was briefly described in the preceding chapter.

The reasons for building COMET reflected a knowledge deficit in that it was intended to replace the sort of human interaction which represented a large proportion of telephone inquiries to the BMA ethics division. The main argument in favour of the use of such a system is to make more readily available the crucial ethical information needed by doctors (Private Conversation with Dr. John Dawson). The implicit disadvantage of not introducing a system like COMET into situations like this is that unethical decisions may be taken simply because the practising doctors do not have ready access to the relevant knowledge.

It is this argument from 'knowledge deficit' that has formed perhaps the strongest argument for the introduction of knowledge-based systems in many varied areas of human activity. In many respects the area of moral reasoning is similar. The introduction of computer-based systems into this area can make the relevant information more widely available and help prevent the sort of erroneous decisions that might be made in the absence of such systems.

This need not necessarily exclude humans from moral decision making. The computer-based system could act as decision support or teacher while in no way supplanting the human decision-maker. This pattern of use of a AI-based moral reasoner is much more attractive in a moral sense because the ultimate responsibility for any decision remains with the human. This is, of course, the case with COMET system where a doctor must accept responsibility for the ethical consequences of his decisions, regardless of the advice he has received from the system.

Some further arguments in favour of developing computer-based moral reasoning systems are based not so much on the claimed ability of the systems as on the perceived inadequacies of human beings. Computer-based systems could offer greater consistency in the application of moral judgements. If all doctors used a computer-based system as the final arbiter on ethical matters then there would at least be standardisation of ethical judgements by the medical profession. Computer-based systems might also be seen as more reliable and less prone to omission than humans, though the reasons for this sort of view are often based upon pre-AI computer systems. AI-based systems, by virtue of the nature of the knowledge they contain and the techniques they use can make many of the same errors as humans. There is some truth in the observation that humans can sometimes be prejudiced and can deceive themselves about the soundness of their judgements, but using this as an argument in favour of replacing them with computer-based systems may stem more from a desire to minimise human participation in this area than from a hope of improving the level of decision-making within it. A compromise position might be to use the computer-based system as a teaching aid to try to improve the level of human performance in moral reasoning.

The most important argument in favour of this sort of work is the need to inject human values into AI systems. The writers who have noted this need (Torrance 1986) are more influenced by the desire to reduce the lack of human values in most present-day AI systems than by the desire to replace human moral reasoning. There are several dimensions to the task of injecting human values into AI systems. One is to prevent those AI systems built solely by engineers in the interests of military and large-scale industrial interests, being rendered dangerous by the narrow range of human values in their knowledge-bases. Another is to facilitate the provision of better human interfaces. That is, to make AI more amenable to users who have and sometimes use moral knowledge. In spite of these noble arguments in favour of the development of computer-based moral reasoners, there are many dangers, considered in the next section.

The Case Against

The picture of a computer-based system being used to support human decision making in the moral area is deceptively positive. There are many reasons why the use of computer-based systems in the moral area should cause concern. At an intuitive level the whole prospect may strike many as distasteful. Most of those who take this view will feel that the best that can be achieved is artificial or simulated moral reasoning. Of course, if one believes, for reasons similar to those mentioned in the penultimate section, that computer-based systems cannot perform genuine moral reasoning, then a strong argument against their use follows from this belief. That is that some sort of devaluation of moral reasoning may be caused by their introduction. According to this view, some gullible people may come to see the artificial sort of moral reasoning performed by such systems as genuine, which would threaten the status of the genuine moral reasoning carried out by human beings.

One counter-argument to this view is provided by the fact that if the reasoning carried out by the computer-based systems were markedly inferior to that carried out by humans this should be immediately apparent. In this case no-one would seriously expect a computer-based moral advisor to produce useful advice and such devices would be mere curiosities. In other words, if one seriously believes that it is impossible to use AI to generate genuine moral knowledge then one can make no argument against doing such research stronger than that it is a waste of money. For the research to be in any sense dangerous or undesirable it has to be successful enough, at least in appearance, to deceive a significant number of people.

Therefore, in order to give a clear argument against research into computer-based moral reasoning it is necessary to accept, at least in principle, the technical possibility of building such systems. It is very important, though sometimes difficult, to separate technical objections from moral objections in this area. The most important conflation of the two types of objection is provided by the argument that whatever computer-based moral reasoning provides is not genuine moral reasoning, but some simulated or lesser form of what humans do when they carry out moral reasoning. The next chapter includes an argument that having lesser orders of morality might itself be morally wrong.

Even allowing the technical possibility that computer-based systems could carry out genuine moral reasoning and that there may be a demand for this sort of system, there are some very strong arguments against building such systems. The first is that it is essential for humans to take responsibility for the moral consequences of their actions. There are great problems in moving responsibility from humans to some sort of artefact. These could be re solved by fully accommodating artefacts within our moral codes (this is more fully discussed in the next chapter); however, there is little prospect of doing this in the foreseeable future.

Another problem is the myth of 'computer infallibility'. Many people do not see computers as prone to the same sorts of errors as human beings. Indeed some people may seem them as unfailingly accurate in their calculations. This is a very dangerous myth in the case of AI-based moral advice. The sort of potential systems which we have been considering would be fallible in the extreme and perhaps dangerously so. It would be working on uncertain information, often by means of techniques which do not yield certainty in conclusions. It would contain little or no common-sense and might well share the human prejudices of its designers. Perhaps worst of all, it would be able to produce detailed justifications of its conclusions when asked. We should all hope that the designers of AI-based moral advisors do not try to exploit the myth of 'computer infallibility' in selling their systems, for this could have unpleasant consequences.

Further arguments against the widespread use of computer-based moral reasoning are provided by the importance of being able to take moral decisions to our view of what it is to be human. To this we might add the notion of 'moral deskilling'. Deskilling is a word that has come to be much used in discussions of the social implications of computers. It denotes the use of computer technology to replace the skilled component of work and thereby to reduce the human working from skilled craftsman to machine minder. The widespread use of computer-based systems to perform moral reasoning would, almost certainly, lead to 'moral deskilling'. Since moral judgements are often extremely difficult for informed and sensitive humans to make, over-reliance on computer-based assistance would be a great temptation. In this way people might gradually lose their ability to make moral judgements.

In some forms of dangerous or unpleasant work we might welcome the gradual replacement of humans; in the area of moral judgement, it might be construed as the loss of a skill that is itself constitutive of being human.

Further problems are raised if we consider the notion of a 'moral community'. That is to say that we may feel that being able to make moral judgements is balanced by being also the subject of moral judgements by others. In this case we may feel that there is an imbalance created if we are to take seriously the judgements of computer-based systems without making them part of the community of beings that we feel have moral worth. As with responsibility, the notion of artefacts having moral worth is too far in the future to distract us here (although it is discussed in the next chapter). This imbalance may well prompt reluctance to allow computer-based systems to give moral advice.

The compromise position that might result in practice is that computer systems may be used to generate moral advice but not to be assigned any moral responsibility. This is a position that I have advocated as necessary to avoid the misuse of all types of knowledge-based systems (Whitby 1988). The problem is that few, if any humans will be able to live up to this principle. People already use computers as an excuse for their own mistakes. This is undoubtedly even more to be expected in the use of moral reasoning systems.

Conclusions

The decision as to whether or not research in this area is morally acceptable is a moral question. It is also, in some ways, a metaethical question[3] since views on the likelihood of success depend upon one's views on the nature of moral judgements. Success in providing a computational account of moral reasoning would be the nearest thing available to empirical proof for those who maintain that morality is, or should be, entirely rational. Those who stress intuitive or spiritual elements in morality would seem bound to oppose the project. An interesting corollary of the argument about 'moral deskilling' is that it should be for individual readers to decide whether the arguments against the use of computer-based moral reasoning outweigh those arguments in favour, as given in the previous section. Whatever you conclude, it should at least be clear that this is not a decision to be made primarily on technical grounds.

On balance it seems to me that the arguments in favour of continuing to research this area outweigh those for neglecting it. The potentially disastrous consequences of trying to represent knowledge such as medical or financial expertise without any consideration of the moral dimensions are even worse than the dangers of introducing computer-based moral reasoning. It is, obviously, something needing much discussion by as wide a group as possible.

Notes

1. Rules here should be read as 'production rules, frames, nets or whatever method of knowledge representation is chosen'.

2. Connectionism or PDP (Parallel Distributed Processing) is a relatively new approach to some of the problems of AI. It involves an approach to computation inspired by some aspects of brain biology. Systems built under this approach (often referred to as neural nets) differ strongly

from conventional AI systems in that they do not represent their knowledge explicitly (in portions of program that can be examined, for example) but rather in the 'activation state' of the entire network. This has the advantage for the present discussion that there is no need to make knowledge explicit in order to represent it within a neural net. Instead the net would be 'trained' on a number of typical examples, until it can respond correctly in a sufficiently high proportion of cases. For more details see, for example, Rumellhart, McClelland, and the PDP Research Group 1986.

3. Metaethics is the branch of moral philosophy which deals with the nature of morality itself - typically discussing question such as the meaning of term such as 'right' and 'good'.

References

Boden, M. (1987) Artificial Intelligence and Natural Man, (2nd ed), London, MIT Press, pp. 298-344 and 493-494.

Charniak, E. and McDermott, D. (1985) Introduction to Artificial Intelligence, Reading, Ma. Addison Wesley, pp. 453-482.

Danielson P. (1992), Artificial Morality, London, Routledge.

Hare, R.M. (1963), Freedom and Reason, Oxford University Press, pp. 10-13.

Lenat, D. (1977), 'The Ubiquity of Discovery' Artificial Intelligence 9pp.257-286.

Lenat, D. (1983), 'the Role of Heuristics in Learning by Discovery: Three Case Studies', in Michalski, R.S., Carbonell, J., and Mitchell, T.M. (eds) Machine Learning: An Artificial Intelligence Approach, Palo Alto, Ca., Tioga.

McClelland, J., Rumelhart, D., and the PDP Research Group, (1986) Parallel Distributed Processing: Explorations in the microstructure of Cognition vol 1, Cambridge, Ma., MIT press.

Penrose, R. (1989), The Emperor's New Mind, Oxford University Press.

Prichard, H.A. (1949), Moral Obligation: Essays and Lectures, Oxford, Clarendon.

Ross, W.D. (1930) The Right and the Good, Oxford, Clarendon.

Searle, J.R. (1984), Minds, Brains, and Science: The 1984 Reith Lectures.

Sieghart, P. and Dawson, J. (1987) 'Computer-aided medical ethics' in Journal of Medical Ethics, 13, pp.185-188.

Torrance, S. (1986), Ethics Mind and Artifice in Gill, K.S. (ed) Artificial Intelligence for Society, Chichester, John Wiley & Sons. p.70.

Whitby, B.R. (1988), AI: A Handbook of Professionalism, Chichester, Ellis Horwood.

Wright, D. (1971), The Psychology of Moral Behaviour, Harmondsworth, Penguin.

The potential Moral Duties and Rights of Intelligent Artifacts

Introduction

The last two chapters deliberately suspended a number of difficult philosophical questions and it is time to confront some of those. In doing so, it is inevitable that the discussion will sometimes concern more distant possibilities, rather than immediate problems raised by new technologies. This should not lead to dismissal of these issues as science fiction or as technically impossible. Whereas the last two chapters were situated firmly in the present, this chapter is more speculative, but only in so far as this is necessary to tie up some of the many loose ends left by the preceding chapters.

Having examined the possibility of advice-giving systems using AI techniques to become artificial moralists which modify, or even generate, moral precepts it is not so large a step to ask questions such as 'how might we build an AI system with a conscience?'. That is not so say that we really need to build such a system, though the previous chapter (Implications of the Computer Representation of Moral Reasoning) suggested some reasons why we might eventually do so. Most of the problems raised in this chapter will have little, if any, effect on ordinary peoples' lives in the foreseeable future. This, however, does not mean that these problems are fanciful, fictitious or irrelevant. It would seem prudent, to say the least, to begin to examine these issues now.

There are a number of reasons for considering these issues before they become matters of urgency. This is an area where the 'powerful ideas' of the first chapter may have the most human of human consequences. The possibility that we may someday be following novel moral precepts that have been generated by entirely artificial means may itself be morally repugnant. In this case, research in this area should be carefully examined, if not controlled. This chapter does not simply propose controls on this sort of research. It is instead an attempt to show that this is a genuine moral question that can be discussed in the same terms as more familiar moral questions.

This is not so simple a task as it might at first seem. Strong opinions and prejudices surround this area. Many people will feel that artifacts of any sort cannot make 'genuine' (whatever that might mean) moral judgements - this is something that only humans can do. At the other extreme, some people will feel that intelligent artifacts will inevitably generate their own moral principles and that these may well be better than those that humans have managed to come up with. To initiate serious discussion of this area it is necessary to argue strongly for a middle view. Suspending, for the moment, the purely technical problems, this chapter will argue that artificially generated moral principles are a serious possibility, but one that we should subject to deep and intense moral scrutiny.

Several other moral problems surround this general area. Among these are the implications of one day building artifacts that have some sort of moral worth. This may well be even more distant than the moral implications of our acceptance of artificially generated moral precepts. However, it has been pointed out (for example in Torrance 1986, LaChat 1986, and Anderson 1989) that some accounts of the goals of AI research have clear and important moral implications. That is to say that if AI is striving to produce artifacts that are 'genuinely conscious' (whatever that might mean) then these artifacts would have a prima facie claim to be worthy of moral consideration by human beings.

There are a number of interesting philosophical questions raised by consideration of the moral worth of artifacts. Not least among these would be the analysis of the expression 'genuinely conscious'. Further questions involve the way in which we attribute moral worth to both humans and non-humans. Many of these questions cannot be given thorough consideration in a single book, let alone one chapter, and will be only briefly touched upon here. One interesting conclusion of this chapter will be to show that consideration of the potential moral duties and rights of intelligent artifacts provides a novel, interesting, and useful approach to this cluster of philosophical questions. It is to be hoped, therefore, that debate will at least be started and that thorough consideration will eventually result.

A final but extremely important introductory point must be made, before proceeding to more detailed consideration of the potential moral duties and rights of intelligent artifacts. This chapter assumes, as have the preceding two chapters, that there is a clear dividing line between natural creatures such as humans on the one hand, and artifacts, such as AI systems, on the other. This assumption may, in all probability, be rendered false by future technological developments. The increasing substitution of artificial devices for parts of human bodies and brains may make this dividing line obscure. Developments in genetic engineering and related technologies hold out the promise (or threat!) that we may one day be able to completely predetermine the genetic make up of a human being or animal. In this case, we might ask whether such a creature being whose genetic structure had been chosen by a computer program without outside supervision, should be considered completely natural or, to some extent, an artifact.

It is convenient, for present purposes, to discuss the problems of the potential moral rights and duties of intelligent artifacts as if they are likely to be raised by a future generation of intelligent robots. However, it is just as probable that the distinction between humans and artifacts will be progressively obscured by developments in genetic and prosthetic technology. This probability does not make the discussion of the moral worth of artifacts misguided; it makes it even more significant.

Why should we discuss Robot Morality?

A good starting point for the discussion of robot morality is the question as to why anyone would want to discuss the notion of an artificial morality at all. One very interesting approach to this issue has been provided by Danielson (Danielson 1992). Danielson's artificial morality is an attempt to demonstrate the rational nature of morality using computational techniques. The overall thesis of Danielson's work is that suitable computer-simulated moral agents can provide a new method for studying the relation between rationality and morality. Of course, as made clear in the preceding chapter, it is more accurate to describe Danielson's project as a programme of research into the principles underlying human morality than as an investigation into what sort of moral principles we might need to build into intelligent artifacts. Nonetheless, it provides a clear example of the way in which serious examination of this area might shed light on familiar problems of human morality.

There are several reasons why this should be the case. There is the somewhat academic argument that simply by thinking about artificial moral problems we may sharpen and refine our ability to deal with real moral problems. There is a more important reason for the consideration of robot morality as opposed to simply any artificial moral problem, however. This stems from the fact that, in theory at least, we know much more about the inner workings of our artifacts than we know about ourselves. This would have the advantage that discussions in the field of robot morality could avoid being detained by the many still unanswered questions of human psychology. It is, for example, notoriously difficult to establish real human needs, although few moral codes can avoid talking of human needs. In the case of artifacts such questioning as to which needs are genuine should much more often have non-controversial answers. There is even the intriguing possibility that some questions about the psychological aspects of moral behaviour could be solved by certain types of AI experiment.

Against this possibility must be weighed the argument that experiments in this area may themselves have unpleasant moral consequences. If any area of AI research merits the discussion of a possible moratorium on research, it is this one. However, even the opposite view entails that widespread informed discussion would be beneficial.

A second reason for giving serious consideration to the area of robot morality is the possibility that it may help us to understand the whole area of non-human morality. There is growing interest in the moral position of animals and obviously there will be parallels between consideration of the moral position of artifacts and of animals. That is not to say that any conclusion reached about the moral status of artifacts can be applied to animals or vice-versa. This second reason merely suggests that consideration of the possibility of non-human morality is a worthwhile intellectual exercise both in the case of animals and artifacts.

The area of robot morality would seem, therefore, an appropriate topic for discussion by philosophers, even if it is not yet a realistic technical possibility. In addition, AI may move into this area by a series of small improvements, rather than a spectacular breakthrough. It is important, therefore, to discuss problems such as those related to robot morality in advance of technical realization. Problems of this sort approach in a gradual rather than spectacular manner.

What sort of cognitive elements would an artifact require in order to be a Moral Agent?

Many readers may feel that any sort of intelligent artifact could not be a moral agent simply because it is an artifact. Because of this, they might say, it should be seen as merely a tool of some human or group of humans. According to this view all artifacts, no matter how sophisticated or autonomous, should be treated as classical machines, such as steam engines. If they contribute in any way to human happiness or misery then their designers, owners, or operators should be praised or blamed accordingly. No praise or blame attaches directly to the artifact.

As one writer (Boden 1981) succinctly points out, one of the reasons that we respect others' interests is precisely because they are human interests. An artifact can only have 'second order human interests', reflecting the goals of its designer. There have been arguments made (for example in Singer 1979) that non-human animals can have interests that we should respect in a similar manner, even if not to an equivalent extent, to the way in which we respect the interests of other human beings. However, there are many problems with extending notions such as praise and blame and moral responsibility to non-human animals and it seems to me that this area sets no useful precedents for artifacts. It would seem that for an artifact, that is something ultimately produced by human activity and for the purpose of furthering those interests, it is safest to ignore any claim to the having of independent interests.

This view has many attractive features. In particular, it is generally desirable to prevent the regrettable human tendency to avoid receiving appropriate blame by hiding behind technology. For this reason alone, it is not morally desirable to encourage ways in which artifacts could share in moral praise or blame with human beings. It is clear that present day AI systems should not share in praise and blame with human beings. However, to resolutely maintain that no artifact ever could, may be little more than blind prejudice.

As AI systems become more sophisticated and play a greater part in the moral life of humans, we may have to slightly modify our views. It is still possible to maintain that an artifact, no matter how sophisticated, could never be a moral agent and could never come to have moral worth. This view, however, could not be based upon any properties which that artifact possessed or lacked. If it is to be maintained about all possible future artifacts, than it can only be based upon the fact that they are artifacts. Some of the ways in which such a position could be supported are discussed in a subsequent section of this chapter 'Possible human reactions to morality for intelligent artifacts'.

If we reject the argument that it is simply the fact of being an artifact that prevents them from having moral rights and duties, then the question posed in the title of this section is a worthwhile one. It should be possible to identify certain features that are possessed by moral agents and which, if somehow built in to or acquired by an artifact would cause it to be or become a moral agent.

Before listing candidates for such features it is worth noting that we are typically extremely vague about whether or not human beings qualify as moral agents. We tend to judge by age and maturity with rather heavy-handed exclusions for the very stupid or very strange. The advent of having to take difficult decisions about the features of artifacts which render them moral agents may make us stricter with humans. This would be an example of a powerful idea emanating from AI affecting a far wider area, in the way described in earlier chapters.

It is also time to remark that so far two distinct questions have been conflated. These are: 'what moral duties might intelligent artifacts eventually have?' and 'what moral rights might intelligent artifacts eventually have?' In the case of human beings the second question is dealt with in a distinctly different way from the first. That is to say that human beings are regarded as having moral rights simply because they are human beings[1]. Human beings are regarded as having moral duties only at those times when they meet a fairly strict set of criteria. These include that the person concerned acted freely and with awareness that they could have acted otherwise.

In the case of artifacts, the position is quite different. There is no case for the automatic acquisition of moral rights as in the case of human beings. Any attribution of moral rights to an artifact needs to be justified in two senses. First, there is the need to show that this artifact meets whatever criteria are proposed for the acquisition of moral rights. Second, there is the need to justify the construction and maintenance of such an artifact.

On the other hand, the notion that an artifact would have some sort of duty to respect the moral rights of human beings (which might or might not be considered a moral duty) needs no such justification. It follows from the moral worth of human beings that we are morally bound not to construct artifacts that act against the interests of human beings. If, as some views of AI promise, we were to construct artifacts that had the power to act against the interests of human beings if they so chose, then we are morally bound to take steps to prevent them doing so.

Arguments might be made that certain types of intelligent artifact could not only acquire moral worth, but also possess moral worth that would, on occasion, be superior to that of some human beings. Some such arguments are considered in the next section. However, these arguments still have to pass the extra test mentioned above, namely: why should we build artifacts that might come to have a moral worth superior to ours?[2]

Putting aside these difficulties there still remains the question as to what features we would need to see in some potential future intelligent artifact in order to describe it in moral terms. If we accept, for the moment, the distinction between moral rights and moral duties in this context, then the problem of moral duties would superficially seem the easiest to resolve. If an intelligent artifact were to be engaged in making decisions that affect humans beings then this ought to be subject to moral scrutiny. If the artifact takes those decisions in an autonomous manner then it would seem reasonable to say that it has moral duties.

This claim needs a little fleshing out. There are already precedents for the moral scrutiny of decisions made by agents that are not human beings. The decisions of a company, committee, and various other forms of organisation can and should be described in this way. The case of the intelligent artifact is slightly different in that it is extremely important to ensure that unscrupulous or weak humans do not hide their own moral duties by attributing them to the artifact. For this reason it is necessary to stipulate that the artifact should be acting autonomously in making the relevant decisions.

In practice, the requirement that an artifact should be acting autonomously is not particularly strict. This would probably entail only that the designers and operators of the artifact could not be expected to anticipate the outcome of its decisions in the relevant cases. This is a feature of conventional computer software that appears to be on the verge of being accepted in law. If we accept this definition of autonomy, and the technical point that designers and programmers cannot anticipate every possible future outcome of the operation of a program, it follows that we could already talk of certain types of software having moral duties.

This might seem too radical a conclusion, partly because of the contrast with the way in which we attribute moral duties to human beings. When we talk of humans having moral duties, we apparently expect considerably more than the definition of autonomy given above. The notion of human moral choice has been discussed at length for at least two millennia. Various differing accounts have been given but some typical human requirements might be that for a given action the human agent could have acted otherwise, was aware of the options available at the relevant time, and freely chose to act as they did. These are difficult requirements to test in the case of human beings (and nowhere near being met by AI systems). What seems more persuasive in the context of the intelligent artifact is that there must be some locus of responsibility. That is to say that if the designers, operators. managers, and other humans cannot be held responsible for its actions, then we should hold the system itself responsible.

There are many problems to be solved and many human attitudes to change in the process of determining how an artifact could be made morally responsible. In the case of human beings we place crucial emphasis on the attribution of praise and blame. As far as I know, there is no AI system that can understand, let alone respond to, praise and blame. It might prove possible to build such a system in the foreseeable future and there are two distinct ways in which this might be tackled.

The first method would be to adopt the knowledge-based approach taken in the last two chapters for advice-giving systems. In this case the effects of praise and blame would have to be formally and explicitly represented within the system. Alternatively we could develop independent and autonomous robots by methods currently being researched, such as 'connectionism' or 'dynamical systems'. The important difference with this approach is that, in any interesting case, it would probably prove impossible to ever determine why the system behaved in a particular way. We may have to accept an approach more heavily biased towards human models of praise and blame if AI develops along this second route, rather than the more explicit knowledge-based route.

All the above bears only upon the question of the circumstances under which intelligent artifacts come to have moral duties. The question of the circumstances under which intelligent artifacts might acquire moral rights may not be so simply answered. We may feel in a rather vague way that if we are prepared to give moral duties to certain types of artifact then it would be appropriate to give them corresponding moral rights. This sort of symmetry might have some justification in the case of human moral rights, but there seems no automatic reason why it should apply in the case of intelligent artifacts.

There are clearly a number of cognitive elements that would provide a prima facie basis for the view that intelligent artifacts should be granted moral rights. The least controversial of these would probably be Bentham's famous claim that the basis of moral worth is the ability to suffer[3]. There are two related problems with adopting this approach to determining whether or not we should grant moral rights to intelligent artifacts.

Assuming, for the moment, that the ability to suffer is the crucial element involved in the ascription of moral worth, then there is an important moral issue raised by our attempting to construct such artifacts. It is certainly debatable as to whether or not such research is morally right. I do not know of any explicit justification for such an aspiration: many writers tend to assume without explicit justification that 'full intelligence', or some such form of words, will simply inevitably involve the ability to suffer. The nature and source of this inevitability remain obscure. If it is inevitable, then the need for serious moral debate at this stage could not be more clear.

The second related problem is that no simple way establishes if the suffering which a system claims, or is claimed, to be capable, is 'genuine' suffering. Many organisms that we believe to be capable of suffering are substantially different from human beings and tend to display their suffering in very different ways. No doubt, there will one day be claim and counter-claim about the genuineness of the suffering of intelligent artifacts. Rather than lay down strict technical or functional criteria for the resolution of this debate at this stage, it seems better to point out that some extreme positions (such as the claim that it is just not possible, or that it doesn't really matter) cannot be reasonably maintained.

It is perhaps as well that no firm conclusions can be drawn on this question. The next section emphasises the role that various human attitudes have to play in determining the answers to most of the questions raised in this chapter. The importance of human attitudes does not mean that we can escape the urgent need to conduct a serious and rational debate on these problems.

Sometimes students leave messages on computer screens that say something like: 'please don't turn me off, I've become conscious'. I have no qualms about turning these machines off; but as I do so I am forced to reflect on the lack of any agreed and effective method of determining under what circumstances such a claim might be well-founded and whether or not we should subject those attempting to construct such a system to moral opprobrium.

Possible Human Responses to Morality for Intelligent Artifacts

In order to discuss these questions in a philosophical, rather than science-fiction manner, it is important to find structures that will limit speculation and focus the debate. One useful way of structuring debate on this subject might be to attempt to categorise the sorts of responses that different people might make to the speculations in the preceding section. This section will criticise six possible human responses.

This analysis makes no claim to sociological accuracy. In practice, people will tend to hold various combinations of response, or to change from one to the other as and when problems are pointed out. However, if we can usefully divide the possible responses to the potential moral rights and duties of intelligent artifacts, a clearer picture of what should be done may, perhaps, begin to emerge.

The Impossibility Thesis

As has already been observed, many people will just not accept that there could ever be a way in which artifacts could come to have moral rights and duties. Confronted by the sorts of examples discussed in the previous two chapters, they would argue that what is being discussed is the use of computer systems to represent, reflect and deliver human morality and not the possibility of some sort of system ever coming to have moral rights and duties in and of itself, and what is more, the very notion is absurd. Of course it is convenient (if highly disingenuous) to avoid discussing a problem by asserting that it impossible. This section (and some subsequent sections) will argue that there are no rational grounds for the claim that the ascription of moral rights and duties to intelligent artifacts is impossible.

One possible reason for the ascription of moral rights and duties to artifacts being seen as impossible is that it might be characterised as clinging to nineteenth century notions of artifacts. Some people will be unhappy with the notion that a machine can take decisions that are not in some way determined by its designer or operator. While this is true of a previous generation of machines, it most certainly is not true of the sort of machines under discussion here. Other writers (eg. Boden 1981, Turkle 1984) have clearly distinguished those concepts of artifact that allow the descriptions in terms of decision-making from those concepts that do not. Some writers have even gone so far as to assert that present-day AI systems could be described as having free will (Anderson 1989). Of course accepting that a machine can make decisions does not entail that we can describe it as having 'free will', nor yet that we should consider ascribing moral duties and perhaps even moral rights to it. Present-day systems have not achieved a level of complexity nor of achievement which would justify talking of them in moral terms, nor of using expressions such as free will. However all that needs to be established here is that there is no impossibility involved.

A second possible reason for the assertion that intelligent artifacts could never come to have moral rights and duties might be that they lack some feature or features generally found in human beings. There are various candidates for such a missing ingredient. A common suggestion, which is analysed in detail in the next section, is that of intuition. Apart from intuition, other possible candidates for such a missing ingredient include emotion, empathy, conscience, creativity, and the soul.

There are two problems with using a missing ingredient argument to assert that it is impossible that intelligent artifacts could ever be ascribed moral duties or rights. The first is that we do not find it necessary to test for any of these ingredients when considering whether animals have moral rights. The second is that, with the possible exception of the soul, there is no reason to believe that it impossible (rather than merely technically difficult) to incorporate these ingredients into a sufficiently sophisticated intelligent artifact. Many AI researchers would regard the incorporation of emotion, creativity, and so on into intelligent artifacts as one of the most exciting challenges of the area. The claim that they must inevitably fail, no matter what techniques they try, is extremely difficult to justify.

On more detailed examination, it is likely that someone advancing the impossibility thesis would be seen to be making one of a number of slightly different claims. Some possible claims are discussed in some of the subsequent sections, in particular 'carbonism', 'intuitionism', and 'two-tier moralities'.

Intuitionism

One difference between human beings and intelligent artifacts that some people might hold to be the basis of a moral difference is a lack of any moral intuition in intelligent artifacts. The important thing about human moral judgements, they would assert, is that human beings possess a special moral sense or intuition that informs (if not determines) their moral judgements. This position needs further analysis since it combines a number of different but relevant claims.

First, there is an established philosophical view that moral judgements are and, more importantly, should be given by our intuitions. According to this view it is the job of the moral philosopher simply to analyse and formalise these intuitions. If we follow this principle in order to decide what should be our reaction to claims that some artifacts should be given moral rights it does not seem effective as a method of resolving the problem. If we have any moral intuitions at all about the prospect of intelligent artifacts being granted moral rights or duties, there seems no good reason to trust those intuitions. This is because we have no experience of the sort of artifact that we need to consider in this context. There is every possibility, therefore, that our intuitions will tend to mislead us.

In an essentially novel area, it is reasonable to expect that intuitions will be unreliable. Moral intuitions will have been built up in familiar cases. In this area that is likely to mean that they may well be based upon concepts of machines that have been described elsewhere in this book as 'nineteenth century'. They will not be based upon concepts of machines that can have purposes and take autonomous decisions. We may come in time to have useful moral intuitions about the sorts of intelligent artifacts that are beginning to be discussed, but there is no reason to assume that anyone has such intuitions yet.

The proponent of intuitionism might accept that the novelty of this area means that we should not trust our moral intuitions, but still claim that the lack of such intuitions was an important difference between intelligent artifacts and humans. This second claim would entail that however intelligent AI systems become and whatever methods they employ for making decisions, for some types of intuitionist those decisions would never become moral decisions, simply because they could not be based on moral intuitions.

In fact, this view might prove most attractive to those who wish to avoid giving serious consideration to the problem of determining any possible moral rights and duties of intelligent artifacts. If one accepts that moral decisions should be based upon purely rational criteria, then it is possible, in principle, for a suitable constructed artifact to take moral decisions. If one wishes to oppose the claim that intelligent artifacts could ever become capable of taking moral decisions then this strand of intuitionism has a superficial appeal.

On further analysis, however, this part of the intuitionist claim cannot dismiss the possibility of intelligent artifacts taking moral decisions. If moral intuition can be analysed, then it is possible that it could, theoretically at least, be incorporated into a suitable AI system. This would certainly be a technological challenge, but it is just the sort of challenge that AI researchers relish. Given success in this endeavour, which is, in principle possible, we could say that the system had an essentially similar set of intuitions to those of a human being in the same situation[4].

If moral intuition cannot, even in principle, be analysed so as to allow the theoretical possibility of incorporating it into an AI system then it can reasonably be dismissed as mystical. In this case it is not capable of supporting a rational argument against the possibility of intelligent artifacts becoming moral agents. Thus intuitionism does not support the impossibility thesis.

Of course, this argument only commits the intuitionist to discussion of the possibility of intelligent artifacts one day being constructed with the right sort of intuitions to become moral agents. Work in this area could accurately be described as being at the stage of pure speculation rather than even the beginning of actual achievement. Genuine espousal of the intuitionist position might entail great enthusiasm for attempts to reproduce moral intuitions in an intelligent artifact. On the other hand, if work in AI suggests that effective moral decision-making is possible without taking account of intuitions, then the claims of the intuitionist about the importance of such intuitions in the case of human moral decision making are greatly weakened.

Moral relativism

In this context, moral relativism can be taken to mean the view that all moral judgements are either purely subjective or culturally relative and that there are no objective values. This is a view that has a certain amount of currency in philosophically illiterate circles, but has little to commend it in this context. According to this view the best response to the moral problems raised by intelligent artifacts would presumably be to wait until it happens and let humans (and presumably suitable artifacts) form their own independent judgements. Since no set of judgements could meaningfully be described as better than any other set of judgements, resolution of the issue would be by means of social power. It follows, therefore, from this view that the sort of analysis undertaken here is pointless.

For this reason, if no other, there is little point in discussing moral relativism further. Indeed one of the conclusions to be drawn from the examination of robot morality might well be that certain meta-ethical theories (of which moral relativism is a paradigm example) have very little to offer as a basis for dealing with future and hypothetical moral problems.

Carbonism

A method of avoiding many of the difficult problems of robot morality would be to assert that only carbon-based life forms can have moral rights and moral duties. According to this view, only human beings and animals could ever be moral agents or have moral duties.

It would certainly be unfashionable (if nothing worse) to argue that moral rights and duties are determined by the possession of a particular type of body chemistry. This would raise overtones of racism and sexism. A possible defence of carbonism might well be mounted by arguing that only God's creations had moral rights and that man's creations could never usurp the unique position of God's creations.

The main problem with this defence is that the distinction between man's creations and God's creations is already problematic and future technological developments may make it even more obscure. If, for example, someone were to succeed in the operation which Moravec (1989) describes of 'downloading' all of a person's mental properties on to a suitable computer, which then went on to claim that it now was that person and therefore entitled to the same moral status as that person when incarnate, the carbonist position might look like unjustified prejudice. I would not wish to suggest that Moravec's operation is likely to become possible, particularly in the rather short time (40 years) that he suggests. However, steady progress in the replacement and supplement of parts of human beings by artificial devices is a serious problem for the hard-line carbonist.

Two-tier moralities

A two-tier morality represents a means of dealing with some of the problems described above. For example we might be tempted to say that intelligent artifacts could have moral duties towards us, but do not have corresponding moral rights. Even more tempting might be the view that the moral considerations we should give to intelligent artifacts is similar, but of a 'lower order' than that which we should give to human beings.

A familiar example of this is provided by Asimov's famous three laws of robotics (Asimov, 1968). Although these three laws have a certain appeal in that they seem to formalise the main requirements of the behaviour of intelligent artifacts towards human beings, they represent a most worrying embodiment of the notion that moral problems can be stated in technical terms. These three laws are quite unlike human laws and seem to be more in line with Asimov's conception of a scientific law. He describes them as 'Built most deeply into a robot's positronic brain'. When the behaviour of robots becomes inconvenient to humans the response is to re-program the robots. The three laws, therefore, have no moral status for humans.

This approach represents a very dangerous model for human morality. There is, to the best of our knowledge, no simple set of three principles that can be programmed into humans to encourage the correct sort of behaviour. The notion that re-programming rather than persuasion, punishment or education should be used in dealing with breaches of codes of behaviour may again be a very dangerous model to adopt in human morality. As intelligent artifacts beome more important in human experience, so the tendency to model our practices on what happens in the artifacts will become more important.

Of course artifacts are different from human and animals, and different in ways that have moral consequences. We should, however, resist most strongly the temptation to reflect those differences in two types of moral codes rather than in different elements of a single moral code. Two-tier moralities tend to devalue both tiers.

Robots' liberation

It is highly probable that some people will sooner or later, argue for the granting of equal moral rights to artifacts in opposition to some of the views described above. It is also probable that some people will espouse this position without waiting for satisfactory answers to the questions concerned with the sort of cognitive elements the robots would require in order to be worth moral consideration. A distinctive feature of the robots' liberation position is that it focuses upon the potential moral rights of intelligent artifacts, rather than upon their moral duties.

As with the other positions on this question, it is necessary to consider this view seriously, partly in order to be able to develop suitable responses to the more extravagant claims that might be made.

The robots' liberation position might be based upon one or both of two distinct claims. First, it might be claimed that it is inevitable that something with sufficient intelligence will eventually perceive its own status and demand equal rights. Second, it might be claimed that the way in which we treat intelligent artifacts reflects upon our own moral worth. Neither of these claims seems adequate to support the position of the robot liberationist.

The essential problem with both of these claims is that we are discussing artifacts. The defining attribute of an artifact is that it is designed and built by human beings, who decide whether, and how, to construct it. There is, therefore, a need to justify the reasons for constructing it in a particular manner. If the sorts of cognitive elements that would render an artifact worthy of moral consideration are simply an inevitable concomitant of the sort of intelligence that AI researchers are trying to achieve, then the whole research program of AI needs examination in moral terms. If these sorts of cognitive elements are 'optional extras' then there is a need to establish a moral justification for including them.

This situation is radically altered once there actually exists an intelligent artifact which might be considered worthy of moral consideration. It follows that arguments against the position of robots' liberation need to be made before it becomes an imminent prospect.

Conclusions

In as much as this discussion suggests any conclusions, they are that there is a need to discuss the moral problems raised by new technologies in this area now. Furthermore, the most consistent and morally desirable way of dealing with these problems is to regard them as a set of moral problems that are contiguous with the areas of human and animal morality. There may be a tendency to see the problems associated with the development of intelligent artifacts as purely technical problems with no more direct moral implications than those involved with developing any sort of computer system. Nothing could be further from the truth. There are some very urgent and difficult moral problems raised by the sort of possibilities discussed in this chapter. It may be too early to propose restrictions on research or too adopt a definite moral position like those discussed above, but, as in so many other areas, the moral problems raised by new technologies can become contemporary social problems with surprising suddenness.

Notes

1. I am aware that there are arguments against this position, but I strongly feel that they are misguided and do not propose to discuss them. Those readers who do not agree with the unsupported claim that all humans automatically have moral worth need not be distracted by this issue as it does not affect the overall argument of this chapter.

2. This is not a rhetorical question. It is, however, extremely difficult to answer usefully. It would seem that the adherents of the view described as 'robot's liberation' in the next section are required to give some sort of answer to this question well in advance of the design of such artifacts. I have yet to hear an answer to this question that does not treat the moral worth of intelligent artifacts as some sort of unintended 'by-product'.

3. In a remarkably far-sighted passage Bentham wrote :

> 'What else is it that should trace the insuperable line? Is it the faculty of reason , or perhaps the faculty of discourse? But a full- grown horse or dog is beyond comparison a more rational, as well as a more conversable animal, than an infant of a day, or a week, or even a month old. But suppose they were otherwise, what would it avail? The question is not, Can they reason? nor Can they talk? but, Can they suffer?.'

[Bentham (1789) *Introduction to the Principles of Morals and Legislation*, Ch.XVIII, Section 1, quoted in Singer 1979]

4. Some hints as to how this might one day be technically possible are given in another part of this book. See the section on 'The semantic deficit' in Chapter 7, 'The Computer Representation of Moral Reasoning'.

References

Anderson, D. (1989) Artificial Intelligence and Intelligent Systems: The Implications, Chichester, Ellis Horwood. pp.163-165.

Asimov, I. (1968) I Robot, St. Albans, Panther Books, pp.43-44.

Boden, M.A. (1981) 'Human Values in a Mechanistic Universe', in Boden, M.A.,Minds and Mechanisms, Brighton, Harvester, pp.265-295.

Danielson, P. (1992) Artificial Morality: Virtuous robots for virtual games, London, Routledge.

LaChat, M. (1986) Artificial Intelligence and Ethics: An Exercise in the Moral Imagination, The AI Magazine, Summer 1986, pp.70-79.

Moravec (1989) Mind Children: the future of robot and human intelligence, Boston Ma., Harvard University Press.

Singer, P. (1979) Practical Ethics, Cambridge University Press. pp 48-71.

Torrance, S. (1986) Ethics, Mind and Artifice. in Gill K. (ed) Artificial Intelligence for Society, Chichester, John Wiley & Sons, pp.55-72.

Turkle, S. (1984) The Second Self: Computers and the Human Spirit, London, Granada, pp.328-338.

The Virtual Sky is not the limit: Ethics in Virtual Reality

What is VR?

Virtual reality (VR) is the name applied to one of the latest trends in high technology research. In essence it is the delivery to a human, or several humans, of the most convincing illusion possible that they are in another reality. This reality exists only in digital electronic form in the memory of a computer or several computers. Hence it is accurately described as 'virtual'. Its reality stems from the convincing nature of the illusion and, most importantly for moral considerations, the way in which human participants can interact with it.

If one were to ask for a demonstration of VR, one would probably be asked to don a strange looking helmet. Inside this helmet would be a number of small screens on which pictures are projected immediately in front of the wearer's eyes. One might also be asked to wear one or more data gloves or similar devices. Like the helmet, these would be generously connected by wires to the associated computing machinery. The function of a data glove is to transmit, as accurately as possible, the movements of the wearer's hand. These movements are fed into the computer, where they are translated into 'actions' (perhaps virtual actions) within the VR. Devices can also be attached to one's legs, though this is less common; users tend to float in a given direction, rather than walk, in present day VR.

The experience of being connected to all this high technology would be (fairly) close to entering another world. One sees this world via the screens within the helmet. Movement of the head and or the eyes is sensed and the pictures appropriately modified enabling one to 'look around' the world. In general, one can move, pick up objects and interact with other characters within this world. These characters can be either computer-generated or other human participants, similarly connected via helmets, data gloves and so on. Within the world a large amount of activity may be possible. Because VR is highly interactive, what actually happens is determined by the user or users. On the other hand, what is possible is determined by the programmer or programmers. This is an important distinction to which we will return.

Many readers may feel that the experience of present-day VR is probably not convincing enough to carry the label 'reality'. Against this argument it must be noted that humans have immense powers of imagination and a willingness to suspend disbelief. In other words the simulated reality does not need to be a perfect simulation in order to for users to come to believe that it is some form of reality.

In addition, the main imperfection in simulation at present comes from the difficulties inherent in presenting a sufficiently convincing computer-generated image. Presenting a convincing visual input to a human being requires a computer that can handle a vast amount of information. This is both difficult and expensive with existing technology. It is now a familiar, but true, cliché to observe that the power and capability of computing machinery is increasing at a tremendous rate. In addition, a wide variety of techniques for producing more convincing VR are currently being researched. It is reasonable to expect, therefore, that in this crucial respect VR will become steadily more convincing.

Of course, this steady improvement will depend on the availability of financial support. This in turn depends on the existing and anticipated applications of VR. The question of what the applications might be is of central importance to any discussion of the ethical implications. While the technology remains a quaint experiment, it raises few, if any, moral problems. If it becomes generally applied, the moral implications will become much more important.

Implications: The Potential Applications of VR

Predictions of the future applications of new technologies are notorious for their inaccuracy. However there is little difficulty in making various predictions about the future of VR. In many respects VR represents a collection of developments of previous technologies rather than complete innovation. Principal among these are simulators, interactive multimedia systems, and computer and arcade games. When a new technology such as VR becomes fashionable, its enthusiasts (and salesmen) may invest a great deal of energy in asserting that it is radically distinct from its technological antecedents. In the case of commercially available systems they have a clear vested interest in doing so. A more realistic approach would stress that most technological innovations, and VR is typical, are a relatively small development and improvement of pre-existing technologies. This approach may also help show the apparent novelty of the moral problems raised to be largely illusory.

One of the major antecedents of VR was work on flight simulation for combat helicopter pilots. VR retains much in common with flight simulation. In particular, it can provide a training environment in which mistakes are less permanent and costly than they would be in reality. This feature will provide a wealth of application areas for VR, quite possibly assisted, by the availability of generous funding for potential military applications. Just as pilots, submarine captains, and tank commanders are today trained in complex simulators they will in the near future be trained in VR. One particular advantage of VR over a simulator in this application is the way in which it can incorporate multiple participants, for example, in competition or in combat with each other. VR is likely to find successful applications in many forms of combat training.

The usefulness of VR in combat training is also accompanied by its applicability in many forms of civilian training. In VR dangerous chemicals and machinery can be handled realistically without physical danger to the user or users. In many situations it is desirable to allow learners to make mistakes and yet protect them from the consequences of those mistakes. This is obviously the case with training for the management of nuclear power stations or dangerous chemical plants. The advantages of using VR instead of a laboratory for teaching physics and chemistry in schools might not be so obvious. Of course, such a virtual laboratory will be limited in its ability to give practical familiarity with the equipment and techniques. However in many areas, the handling of radioactive and other dangerous materials being a conspicuous example, it will have clear advantages.

Even less obvious may be the usefulness of using VR to let users 'enter' a period of history. This would provide a useful way of teaching history, either in a school or a museum. The use of VR is already proving of interest to creative artists. Anne Barclay Morgan (Barclay Morgan 1992) has pointed out that VR (or cyberspace as it is sometimes called in this area) is a medium that offers possibilities such as interactive paintings and sculptures and plots that can be changed by the audience.

In addition to training and the acquiring of factual information VR will provide a useful tool for education. It is, in many ways, the ultimate development of Seymour Papert's 'microworlds' (Papert 1980). The attractions of being able to learn through doing, particularly in co-operation with others, will soon be seen by educators.

Another major area where VR will sooner or later find successful application is in the field of entertainment. This again, is an application area which is essentially an extension of existing technologies and practices. Just as the flight simulator can be seen as a training precursor of VR, so can the cinema, video game, and computer-game be seen as entertainment precursors of VR. Already arcade games are moving towards military VR in terms of the realism of their displays and the richness of possible interactions. As the technology improves there will be a strong market for VR in arcade and home entertainment.

The development of the entertainment market depends on the technology achieving a sufficiently low cost and this may take slightly longer than the developments discussed in the last couple of paragraphs. However, there is every good reason to believe that VR used for entertainment will become commonplace within a few years. Two routes of development are possible. First, relatively low-tech, low-cost VR could become available for use in the home. Second, relatively high-tech, high-cost VR might be set up in population centres and hired by the minute by large numbers of users. These two routes are not mutually exclusive and may well be able to co-exist, just as at present many people both visit the cinema and own a video player.

Putting these two applications together produces the rather depressing conclusion that VR will also be used for advertising. The fact that there is almost literally a captive audience to which information can be delivered with convincing realism, yet with no test of truthfulness, will make VR just too good to miss for the advertiser. VR that claims to give the experience of driving the latest sports car, complete, no doubt, with admiring crowds who all seem to know one's name, will abound. The need for ethical, and legislative, controls on this application of VR should be obvious.

There can be little doubt that VR will become widespread in training, entertainment, and advertising applications. Probably most worries over their moral implications will be expressed in the context of entertainment, rather than the other application areas. However, there is a need for moral scrutiny in all three areas.

In the case of training, those designing the VR will probably have clearer objectives and may well, therefore, limit the possibilities open to the user accordingly. There is also likely to be some monitoring, even if it is just some sort of final examination, of the users of training VR. This monitoring provides at least some control over possible misuse and bad outcomes for the users of training VR.

In the case of advertising there is an obvious need to prevent the user of VR becoming a victim of intrusive advertising and to ensure that the advertising does not give a totally false impression of the value of the product to him. This may prove somewhat more difficult in the case of VR than in television or film because of the ability of a VR designer to tailor the advertising to the needs and desires of an individual. The present-day advertiser tends to work with media that are aimed at groups of potential customers. A VR designer, by contrast, can easily take account of choices made by a user and use those choices to target more effective advertising techniques at a particular individual.

However, there are codes of practice in place for television and film and there is no obvious reason why these should not be immediately extended to cover VR. In the light of the sort of problem discussed in the last paragraph, improvements to these codes may well prove desirable. It is important to recognize that this constitutes no argument against using what already exists now.

Most public concern is likely to be voiced with respect to the use of VR in entertainment. The following section will therefore take the entertainment applications of VR as typical, though the conclusion will attempt to draw all three application areas together. It is the entertainment application area that is most likely to be experienced by the general public. In addition, there are important ways in which the use of VR in entertainment is likely to be less tightly controlled than in training. On the other hand, it would seem that with VR as entertainment the sky is the limit.

The Ethical Implications of VR

Doubts have been voiced about the implications of the sort of freedom that can be provided by VR. In particular, there are worries about users having the freedom to commit rape and murder within VR. Before examining such worries in detail it is worth observing that this is an ethical rather than technical issue. It is technically possible to construct VR in such a way that almost every possibility of the user's imagination can be fulfilled. It is also possible for designers to place arbitrary limits on what is possible within a particular VR. They could, for example, simply set up a VR in such a way that killing, rape, and many other morally proscribed actions are impossible. They could even set up VR in which some form of punishment (virtual or real) was the consequence of attempting to commit a proscribed action within that VR. It is also worth observing that this issue needs to resolved in the immediate future since the existence of VR that allows killing or similar morally reprehensible acts will itself constitute a powerful argument against those who want to place some sort of restriction upon VR.

These are exciting, intriguing, but dangerous possibilities. When new technologies raise ethical problems in this way, misunderstandings are often generated. It is easy, for example, to assume that the novelty of the technology is, or perhaps ought to be, reflected in the novelty of the moral issues surrounding it. This is unlikely to be the case, as will be argued in the following sections.

A second group of misunderstandings stems from the fact that moral principles and beliefs are seen to be in a state of flux. The new possibilities opened up by technologies such as VR may heighten anxieties about this. In a philosophical overview of this area Colin Beardon (Beardon 1992) has argued that the emergence of VR is related to a contemporary crisis in philosophy. There is evidence that philosophical problems are raised by VR. In particular, VR (at least in its most hyped versions) closely resembles the philosophers' notion of 'the experience machine'(Nozick 1974, Glover 1984). Beardon is correct to point out that debates about VR can aggravate cultural and philosophical splits in contemporary society, however this chapter takes his conclusion that the best response to this is a pragmatic one.

It is sometimes even argued that morality itself no longer has any meaning with the rise of modern secular societies. To a certain extent it is simply the case that morality has always been in a state of flux. That is to say that there is a process of general debate on moral questions that probably rarely approaches consensus. This is not the place to attempt in any way to expand on this sort of debate. Instead it will be argued that there is an immediate need to resolve certain questions about what is morally acceptable in VR. These questions can be resolved by applying familiar principles. The doubts mentioned at the start of this section are about the impact of VR on human beings and the debate is therefore easiest to resolve when seen as a continuation of similar debates about the impact of older technologies on human beings.

A further group of misunderstandings surrounds questions who should take responsibility for discussing and resolving the moral questions surrounding new technology. The usually unjustified belief on the part of laymen that they are incapable of understanding the technology makes them reluctant to enter the debate. The sometimes unjustified belief on the part of technologists that moral questions are something they neither know nor care about makes them reluctant to start such debates. The position is further complicated by the fact that those designers of VR who set themselves high ethical standards need support, preferably from the public at large. Without this, they will not be able counter the arguments of customers or managers who demand morally dubious features in VR. A less satisfactory, but more practical alternative may be to form professional organizations and draw up codes, as has been done with many other forms of technology. However this takes time and there is a certain urgency to these matters.

Virtual Reality: The Case for Restrictions

VR is a technology which can offer significant benefits in training applications. In entertainment, it is probable that we could feel at least as positive about VR as we do about visual art or cinema, for example. In addition there are a number of arguments related to traditional views of the the freedom of the individual. These take as central the technical claim that what happens within a VR is truly private, (at least in the case where there is only a single user). If one believes that individuals should be free to do absolutely anything which does not affect the freedom of others, then a VR would seem to be the ideal place to do such things.

It may not always be completely true that others' freedoms are unaffected by what one does within VR. In a multi-user competitive VR, winning will involve someone else losing, for example. It is important not to confuse this issue. What one does within a single-user VR does not directly affect others and can therefore be regarded as private. Indirect effects will be considered in the following.

In a multi-user VR, one can carry out actions that directly affect other users, firstly in a virtual sense. The virtual nature of these actions clearly reduces their moral significance, but may not completely remove it. The degree to which a virtual offence is morally reprehensible depends on (among other things) its believability to the user against whom it is committed. This would seem to be an area where empirical research is needed.

Not all the offences that might be committed within a VR are necessarily virtual in the above sense. The nature of interaction in a multi-user VR renders physical offences virtual in this sense, but there is a whole range of non-physical offences, such as slander, libel, and verbal degradation that is just as real when committed within a VR. This is another area where the correct moral response is not difficult, but there is some urgency in ensuring that existing provisions are extended to cover the area of VR.

A more difficult set of moral problems is raised by the case of the single-user VR. If we are to deal with these problems, we need a clear account of the moral status of immoral behaviour within a VR, even when no other person is directly affected by that behaviour.

The first pragmatic step toward such an account must be to once again deny the claim that the technology makes any fundamental difference to the moral problems involved. The moral questions are to be resolved solely by consideration of the effects of the technology upon human beings. The complexity or novelty of the technology is of no concern, other than its tendency to obscure these effects. In considering the moral problems raised by VR, therefore, we are considering human problems only. Technological questions are merely a fog surrounding those problems.

A further step in clarification is to recall that VR has important overlaps with older technologies. Discussion of its moral implications, therefore, can draw on many existing notions. There is no need to return to fundamental moral principles in order to deal with most of the issues raised by VR.

There seem to be four main arguments for the restriction of certain types of activity within VR. Those clamouring for restrictions on VR may combine these arguments in practice. A clearer picture of their validity is likely to emerge from detailed and separate examination:

1) 'They might do it for real'

This argument suggests that people who regularly perform morally reprehensible acts such as rape and murder within VR are as a consequence more likely to perform such acts in reality. This is certainly not a new departure in the discussion of ethics. In fact the counter argument to this suggestion is at least as old as the third century BC. It is based on the Aristotelian notion of catharsis (Aristotle 1968). Essentially, this counter argument claims that performing morally reprehensible acts within VR would tend to reduce the need for the user to perform such acts in reality.

The question as to which of these two arguments is correct is a purely empirical one. Unfortunately, it is not clear what sort of experiment could ever resolve the issue. A high correlation, for example, between those who perform rape and murder in VR and those who do it in reality does not establish any causal link. It may be that there is a level of motivation to perform morally reprehensible acts in some individuals that even the most effective catharsis cannot assuage.

A high correlation of this sort can therefore be interpreted in two completely different ways. On the one hand it might be seen as an indication that the use of VR had delayed the real performance of the morally reprehensible act. On this view the pressure to perform such acts might sometimes become too great for the cathartic effect of VR to work. On the other hand, the correlation might be interpreted as showing that performing events in VR often leads to performing them in reality. There is little prospect of resolving this debate in a scientific fashion.

However, it would be extremely foolish to dismiss this argument simply because we can see no way of testing its major claim. With many Western societies showing both a rise in civil violence and crime and an increase in the portrayal of such actions by entertainment media, there is at least the possibility of a causal link. There is also a possibility that VR might pose more of problem than previous more passive media. This is because it involves physically 'practising', in an important sense, the morally reprehensible acts that we would not wish performed in reality. It may well be the case that some of behavioural conditioning can therefore be produced more readily by VR than by previous technologies. If there is such a process, there should already be reliable, but secret, data emerging from the area of military training. Perhaps a 'peace dividend' for psychological researchers could be in the form of unrestricted access to this data.

The difficulty of resolving the empirical questions should not cause us to ignore the problem. Morally speaking, it behoves scientists to commit a vast research effort to devising some way of answering these empirical questions. In the absence of such hard evidence, many people will simply assume that the answers to the empirical questions must be in line with their personal prejudices. A more realistic response to this argument is that, not only do we not know at present, but we are not sure how to find out. The present state of knowledge, therefore, entails that this argument, in isolation, will not justify restrictions on VR.

2) 'Some things are not acceptable even in private'

This argument rejects the traditional claims of personal freedom. According to the proponents of this argument, one simply does not have the right to perform morally reprehensible acts, even if no-one else will be affected by them. In other words, it is the sheer unpleasantness of an individual's actions that render them morally acceptable, even if they have no consequences whatsoever. Another way in which this might be interpreted is as having a moral duty to oneself.

The counter to this argument is the libertarian tradition on which most Western secular societies are based. Its classical expression is in J.S.Mill's *On Liberty*:

> The only part of the conduct of anyone, for which he is amenable to society, is that which concerns others. In the part which merely concerns himself, his independence is, of right, absolute. Over himself, over his own body and mind, the individual is sovereign. (Mill 1859 p.14)

The widespread influence of views similar to Mill's is likely to form the basis of opposition to any restriction on VR based on this argument. It must be concluded, therefore, that this argument alone does not justify any restriction on the use of VR.

However, it is worth noting that Mill and most authorities in the libertarian tradition specifically exclude children from the claim of individual authority. This exclusion is reflected in the existing censorship provisions for media such as television and film. Even if video games have unfortunately slipped through this censorship net, there is an immediate need to extend provisions for the protection of children to the technology of VR.

3) 'People will prefer the virtual to the real'

According to one version of this argument, many people will become so entranced by VR that they will avoid the less compliant and enjoyable real world. VR will therefore become the ultimate opiate. If one believes that this will apply to a significant number of people for a significant proportion of their time, VR will be a threat to the fabric of society. Depending on just how convincing one feels the technology will eventually become, this argument gains plausibility from the possibility of spending time in a 'world' where everything can be just as one wants it - rather than the way it is.

One detailed treatment of this sort of argument (Frude 1983) has been made in relation to technologies that promise less than VR. This is discussed elsewhere (Whitby 1988) and need not be repeated here. Instead, it is worthwhile to continue the theme of observing that, despite the excitement and hype, VR is not the first technology to offer this possibility. In fact, in relation to this possibility, VR is simply the latest development in a tradition which goes at least as far back as prehistoric cave-painting. Escapist literature, films, plays and even unaided fantasy are all capable of distracting our attention and interest from reality. VR is a (possibly) more effective way of doing this.

Thus this argument is also unconvincing in isolation. Many new technologies, in particular television, have been cast as a threat to the fabric of society. Society, however, continues more or less successfully in spite of the amount of time that many people spend watching television. There is every good reason to believe that mature people can allocate their time between entertainment and work to the detriment of neither.

A further strong counter to this argument is seen when we consider its policy implications. If some people consistently find VR more attractive than 'real reality' then can it be morally correct to act so as to deny them this alternative? Surely, the morally correct course of action is to pursue ways in which 'real reality' can be made more attractive to them. If their choice is rational, then any attempt to deny them their preference represents the infliction of unnecessary suffering.

4) 'The designers of VR can signal social approval and disapproval'

This argument takes note of the fact that what people generally do within a VR may come to be seen as acceptable in some sense. Thus the designers of VR have the ability to provide a degree of social approval or disapproval for the categories of actions that they allow within a VR: recall that what is possible within a VR is determined by its designers. They have it within their power to reward morally reprehensible behaviour, to prevent morally reprehensible behaviour, or to punish it.

Many examples of rewarding morally reprehensible behaviour are provided by the current crop of arcade games. These require and encourage a level of simulated violence that would be unacceptable in reality. The designers of these games need to examine their consciences! The marketing success of these games, particularly among the young, is a gloomy portent of what might be expected from crude home-entertainment VR.

The designer of VR could just as easily prevent a user from engaging in morally reprehensible acts by simply not allowing murder, rapes, and the like to happen with the VR, or by automatically ejecting the user who attempted to commit such acts. Similarly, there would be no technical problem in providing for a suitable 'virtual punishment' for users who attempt to commit various morally reprehensible acts within VR. The moral implications of these technical possibilities are discussed in the next section.

This argument seems much more convincing than the previous three. Even in the absence of evidence that users are more likely to commit morally reprehensible acts in practice, drop out of real interactions, and so on, there is no doubt that legitimacy is given to actions by one being encouraged to perform them within VR.

This argument is undoubtedly the most persuasive case for restriction upon VR. However, people may consider that it is not entirely practical. The existence of, and demand for, extreme violence in computer and arcade games may seem to put irresistible pressure on VR designers to allow a similar frequency of killing and maiming. The survival of the pornography industry in spite of legal restriction, suggests that there will inevitably be virtual pornography, even if underground.

These practical problems are not an effective counter to this argument, since it is important to show approval and disapproval of certain activities, even if these standards are not always attained in practice. Ultimately, much depends on the attitude of VR designers. It should be clear that they carry a burden of moral responsibility and need to ensure that they set themselves the highest possible standards.

Conclusion: Ethical Virtual Reality

Irrespective of the problems (both practical and philosophical) involved there is a need for urgent action to discuss and identify the ethical issues surrounding VR. The pace of development of modern technology can frequently prove too fast for a leisurely academic development of a philosophical and moral position. The proliferation of computer games that encourage extreme violence, for example, seems to have taken place in advance of widespread social debate[1].

Urgency in and of itself need not entail poorly thought out responses. This chapter makes two, fairly simple, practical suggestions. First, there is the immediate need to extend the age-based censorship on media such as film and television to all forseeable interactive media, including VR. Second, it encourages public (which might entail legislative) support for VR designers in establishing high ethical standards in their work. More might well be needed, but there are greater dangers in procrastination than in partial action.

Solving the immediate problems is, of course, a beginning rather than a conclusion to debate on the ethics of VR. That is an inevitable consequence of the nature of morality. Since morality entails unconstrained choices by human agents, the idea of a code (or any similar device) removing the need to think through the moral implications of our choices is impossible.

This observation applies equally to the idea that VR designers can simply outlaw immoral behaviour within their system. Since the users are effectively denied the choice of whether or not to behave in a moral fashion, their behaviour cannot therefore be described as moral. Ideally, therefore, VR should allow users to behave in ways as wicked or as saintly as are possible in reality. Ideally again, the consequences of those behaviours should be as close as possible to reality. To constrain VR users is to deny them the chance to be moral within VR. It should be noted that this neutral position is most certainly not attained by the current crop of arcade games, that allow a user to indulge in extreme violence against the person without experiencing any of its adverse consequences.

So far it may seem that there has been a concentration on the detrimental moral implications of VR. It is necessary to redress this by pointing out there are many positive moral implications too. VR can, and with any luck will, be used to train and explore positive moral interaction.

Moral philosophers have already begun to explore the use of simulated agents in a 'virtual world' to test the rationality of moral theories and behaviour (Danielson 1992). This could be developed in fascinating ways through the technical possibilities of VR. In particular, VR could be used as a medium in which to explore the consequences of various types of behaviour. Theorists of behaviour could use this as an experimental technique to refine views on exactly how and when humans behave as they do. Theorists of morality could use them in a vast development of Danielson's work to explore the consequences of partial and widespread adoption of various ethical standards. Finally, and perhaps most importantly, the facility to have a reasonable simulation of another's experiences could refine the human ability to empathize. That is to say that the use of VR to give, for example, the experience of crime from the point of view of the criminal, victim, legislator, and law-enforcer might give us all a technologically-based route to far greater moral sensibility.

Notes

1. This implies no criticism of those who determinedly opposed 'shoot-em-up' games in the early 1980s.

References

Aristotle (1968) The Poetics, in Lucas D.W.(ed), Aristotle, OUP.

Barclay Morgan, A. (1991) Interactivity: From Sound to Motion to Narrative, in Art Papers, Vol. 15 No.55. Sept./Oct. 1991.

Beardon C. (1992) The Ethics of Virtual Reality, Intelligent Tutoring Media, Vol. 3, No. 1. pp.23-27.

Danielson, P. (1992) Artificial Morality, London, Routledge.

Frude, N. (1983) The Intimate Machine, New York, New American Library.

Glover, J. (1984) What Sort of People Should There Be?, Harmondsworth, Penguin, pp.92-113.

Mill, J.S., (1859) On Liberty, reprinted in John Stuart Mill A Selection of his Works, Robson J.M.(ed) (1966), Toronto, Macmillan, p14.

Nozick, R. (1974) Anarchy, State and Utopia, New York, Basic Books,pp.42-45.

Papert, S. (1980) Mindstorms: Children , Computers, and Powerful Ideas, New York, Basic Books.

Whitby, B. (1988) Artificial Intelligence: A Handbook of Professionalism, Chichester, Ellis Horwood.

Bibliography

Abelson, R.P. (1973) 'The Structure of Belief Systems' in Schank, R.C and Colby, K.M. (eds) Computer Models of Thought and Language, San Francisco, Freeman.

Adams R., Caruthers J., and Hamil S. (1991) Changing Corporate Values, London, Kogan Page.

Anderson, A.R. (ed)(1964) Minds and Machines, Englewood Cliffs N.J., Prentice-Hall.

Anderson, D. (1989) Artificial Intelligence and Intelligent Systems: The Implications, Chichester, Ellis Horwood.

Aristotle (1968) The Poetics, in Lucas D.W.(ed) Aristotle, Oxford University Press.

Asimov, I. (1968) I Robot, St. Albans, Panther Books.

Association for Computing Machinery Bylaw 19 'Code of Professional Conduct'.

Barclay Morgan, A. (1991) Interactivity: From Sound to Motion to Narrative, in Art Papers, Vol. 15 No.55. Sept./Oct. 1991.

Beardon C. (1992) The Ethics of Virtual Reality, Intelligent Tutoring Media, Vol. 3, No. 1.

Bennun, M.E. (ed) (1991) Computers, Artificial Intelligence and the Law, Chichester, Ellis Horwood.

Bobrow, D.G and Hayes, P.J. (eds)(1985), Artificial Intelligence - where are we?, Artificial Intelligence 25, pp. 413-415.

Boden, M.A. (1977) Artificial Intelligence and Natural Man, Harvester, Brighton.

Boden, M.A. (1981) Minds and Mechanisms, Brighton, Harvester.

Boden, M.A. (1986) Artificial Intelligence and Natural Man, (2nd ed), London, MIT Press.

Boden, M.A. (1990) The Creative Mind, Myths and Mechanisms, Weidenfield and Nicholson, London.

Boden, M.A. (1996) The Philosophy of Artificial Life, Oxford University Press.

Bringsjord, S. (1995) Could, How Could We Tell if, and Why Should - Androids Have Inner Lives, in Ford, K. , Glymour C. and Hayes, P.J. (eds) Android Epistemology, Cambridge Ma., MIT Press, pp.93-121. British Computer Society, Handbook: Code of Conduct, London, BCS Publications.

British Computer Society, Handbook 6: Code of Practice, London, BCS Publications.

British Medical Association (1984) Handbook of Medical Ethics, London, BMA Publications.

Brooks, R. (1992), Artificial Intelligence and Real Robots in Varela, F.J. and Bourgine, P. (eds) Towards a Practice of Autonomous Systems, Proceedings of the First European Conference on Artificial Life, Boston, Ma., M.I.T. Press.

Browne J. and Taylor A. (1989) The Inherent Dangers of 'Naive' Legal Knowledge Bases, AISBQ 68.

Cavalier, P. and Singer, P (1993) The Great Ape Project, Equality beyond Humanity, London, Fourth Estate.

Charniak, E. and McDermott, D. (1985) Introduction to Artificial Intelligence, Reading Ma., Addison Wesley.

Clark, A. and Millican, P. (1996) (eds) Essays in Honour of Alan Turing, Oxford University Press (in press).

Cliff, D., Harvey, I., and Husbands, P. (1993) Explorations in evolutionary robotics. Adaptive Behaviour 2, pp.73-110.

Colby, K.M., Hilf, F.D., Sylvia Weber, and Kraemer, H.C. (1972) Turing-Like Indistinguishability Tests for the Validation of a Computer Simulation of Paranoid Processes in A.I., 3 pp.199-222.

Cooley, M. (1987) Architect or Bee? The Human Price of Technology, London, Hogarth Press.

Council for Science and Society (1989) Benefits and Risks of Knowledge Based Systems, OUP.

Crane, T. (1995) The Mechanical Mind, Harmondsworth, Penguin.

Danielson, P. (1992) Artificial Morality, London, Routledge.

Dennett, D.C. (1991) Consciousness Explained, Harmondsworth, Penguin.

Ennals, R. (1986) Star Wars: A question of initiative, Chichester, John Wiley & Sons.

Erman D., Williams M., and Gutierrez C. (1990) Computers, Ethics and Society, OUP.

Feigenbaum, E.A. (1993) Tiger in a Cage , Distinguished Lecture Series VI, Stanford, University Video Communications.

French, R. (1996) in Clark, A. and Millican, P. (eds) (1996) op.cit.

Frude, N. (1983) The Intimate Machine, New York, New American Library.

Gill K.S. (ed) AI & Society, The Journal of Human and Machine Intelligence, London, Springer-Verlag.

Gill, K.S. (ed) (1986) Artificial Intelligence for Society, Chichester, John Wiley and Sons.

Glover, J. (1984) What Sort of People Should There Be?, Harmondsworth, Penguin.

Goldschlager, L. and Lister, A. (1988) Computer Science: a Modern Introduction, Hemel Hempstead, Prentice Hall.

Hare, R.M. (1963), Freedom and Reason, Oxford University Press.

Harvey, I., Husbands, P., Cliff, D., Thompson, A., and Jakobi, N.(1996) Evolutionary Robotics the Sussex Approach, in Robotics and Autonomous Systems, in press.

Hill, C.P. (1961) British Social and Economic History 1700-1939, London, Edward Arnold.

Hodges, A. (1983) Alan Turing , The Enigma of Intelligence, London, Unwin.

Hofstadter, D.R. and Dennett, D.C.(eds) (1981), The Mind's I, Brighton, Harvester.

Jackson, P. (1968), Introduction to Expert Systems, Addison Wesley, Wokingham.

Kaldor, N. and Mirrlees, J.A.(1961-2) Growth Model with Induced Technical Progress, in Sen (ed) (1970) op. cit. pp. 343-366.

Kuhn, T.S. (1970) The Structure of Scientific Revolutions, (2nd ed.), University of Chicago Press.

von der Leith Gardner, A. (1984), An Artificial Intelligence Approach to Legal Reasoning, dissertation published by Dept. of Comp. Science, Stanford University.

LaChat, M. (1986) Artificial Intelligence and Ethics: An Exercise in the Moral Imagination, AI Magazine, Summer 1986, pp.70–79.

Leith, P (1986) Fundamental Errors in Legal Logic Programming, The Computer Journal, Vol 29, no 6 1986.

Lenat, D. (1977), 'The Ubiquity of Discovery' Artificial Intelligence 9pp.257-286.

Lenat, D. (1983), 'the Role of Heuristics in Learning by Discovery: Three Case Studies', in Michalski, R.S., Carbonell, J., and Mitchell, T.M. (eds) Machine Learning: An Artificial Intelligence Approach, Palo Alto, Ca., Tioga.

LEXIS Handbook (1981) London, Butterworth Telepublishing.

Lucas, J.R. (1961) 'Minds Machines and Godel' in Philosophy Vol. XXXVI, pp. 112-27.

Lycan, W.G.(ed)(1990) Mind and Cognition: A Reader, Oxford, Blackwell.

Lyon, D. (1986) The Silicon Society, Tring, Lion.

Mackie, J.L. (1977) Ethics, Inventing Right and Wrong, Harmondsworth, Penguin.

Macintyre, A. (1968), A Short History of Ethics, London, Routledge and Kegan Paul.

McClelland, J., Rumelhart, D., and the PDP Research Group, (1986) Parallel Distributed Processing : Explorations in the microstructure of Cognition vol1, Cambridge, Ma., MIT press.

McDermott, D.A. (1987). A Critique of Pure Reason Computational Intelligence 3 151-160.

Mahalingham, I (1991) Computer in Law – Hard Cases in Narayanan and Bennun (eds) (1991) op. cit.

Meltzer, B. & Michie, D. (eds.) Machine Intelligence 5, Edinburgh University Press.

Michie. D. (1986) On Machine Intelligence (2nd ed.), Chichester, Ellis Horwood.

Michie, D. (1996) in Clark, A. and Millican, P. (eds) (1996) op.cit.

Mill, J.S., (1859) On Liberty, reprinted in John Stuart Mill A Selection of his Works, Robson J.M. (ed) (1966) Macmillan, Toronto, p14.

Miller, P.L. (1984) A Critiquing Approach to Expert Computer Advice: Attending, Boston Ma., Pitman.

Miller, P.L. (1986) Expert Critiquing Systems, New York, Springer-Verlag.

Minsky, M.L. (1968) Semantic Information Processing, Boston, Ma., MIT Press,p.v.

Minsky, M.L. (1974) A Framework for Representing Knowledge, M.I.T. AI Lab Memo No 306.

Mondey, D. (ed)(1977) The International Encyclopaedia of Aviation, London, Octopus.

Moore, G.E. (1903) Principia Ethica, Cambridge University Press.

Narayanan, A. and Bennun, M.(eds) (1991) Law, Computer Science, and Artificial Intelligence, New Jersey, Ablex.

Nilsson, N.J. (1984) Artificial Intelligence, Employment, and Income in Trappl (ed), (1985), Impacts of Artificial Intelligence, Amsterdam, North Holland.

Nilsson, N.J. (1995) Eye on the Prize, AI Magazine, Summer 1995 pp.9-17.

Nozick, R. (1974) Anarchy, State and Utopia, New York, Basic Books.

O'Shea T. and Self J. (1983) Learning and Teaching with Computers, Brighton,Harvester Press.

Oakley, B. and Owen, K. (1989) Alvey: Britain's strategic Computing Initiative, Cambridge Mass., MIT Press.

Papert, S. (1980) Mindstorms: Children , Computers, and Powerful Ideas, New York, Basic Books.

Partridge, D. (1986) Artificial intelligence: applications in the future of software engineering, Chichester, Ellis Horwood.

Penrose, R. (1989), The Emperor's New Mind, Oxford University Press.

Phillips, P. and Dawson, J. (1985) Doctors' Dilemmas: Medical Ethics and Contemporary Science, Brighton, Harvester.

Prichard, H.A. (1949), Moral Obligation: Essays and Lectures, Clarendon, Oxford.

Quillian, M.R. (1968) Semantic Memory in Minsky, M (ed) (1968) op. cit. pp.227–70.

Rogers, I. (1984) AI as a dehumanizing force in Yazdani and Narayanan (eds) op. cit. pp.222-233.

Ross, W.D. (1930) The Right and the Good, Oxford, Clarendon.

Ryle, G. (1949) The Concept of Mind, London, Hutchinson.

Schank, R.C. and Abelson, R.P. (1977), Scripts, plans goals and understanding, New Jersey, Lawrence Erlbaum.

Schank, R.C. (1986) Explanation Patterns, London, Lawrence Erlbaum.

Schumpeter, J.(1934) The Theory of Economic Development, Harvard University Press.

Searle, J.R. (1984), Minds, Brains, and Science: The 1984 Reith Lectures, Harmondsworth, Penguin.

Searle, J.R. (1994) The Rediscovery of the Mind, Cambridge, Mass. MIT Press.

Sen, A. (ed),(1970) Growth Economics, Harmondsworth, Penguin.

Sergot, M.J., Sadri, F., Kowalski, R.A., Kriwaczek, F. Hammond, P. and Cory, H.T. (1986) The British Nationality Act as a logic program, Communications of the ACM 29 (5), pp.370-386.

Shortliffe, E.H. (1976), Computer-Based Medical Consultations: MYCIN, New York, Elsevier.

Sieghart, P. and Dawson, J. (1987) 'Computer-aided medical ethics' in Journal of Medical Ethics 13, pp.185-188.

Singer, P. (1979) Practical Ethics, Cambridge University Press.

Sloman (1978) The Computer Revolution in Philosophy, Brighton, Harvester.

Smith, B.L. (1985), The Limits of Correctness, Presented at the Symposium on Uninentional Nuclear War, 5th Congress of the International Physicians for the Prevention of Nuclear War, Budapest June 1985.

Susskind, R.E. (1987) Expert Systems in Law, Oxford, Clarendon Press.

Torrance, S. (1986) Ethics Mind and Artifice in Gill, K.S. (ed) (1986) op. cit.

Turing, A.M.(1950) 'Computing Machinery and Intelligence', Mind, vol.LIX,No. 236. pp.433-460 .

Turkle, S. (1984) The Second Self: Computers and the Human Spirit, London, Granada.

Weizenbaum, J. (1966), 'ELIZA - A Computer Program For the Study of Natural Language Communication Between Man and Machine' Communications of the A.C.M., vol.9 no.1 pp.36-45.

Weizenbaum, J.(1984) Computer Power and Human Reason, Handmondsworth, Penguin.

Wenger E. (1987) Artificial Intelligence and Tutoring Systems, Los Altos, Ca., Morgan Kaufmann.

Whitby, B. (1984), 'A.I.: some immediate dangers' in Yazdani and Narayanan (eds) (1984) op.cit. pp. 235-236.

Whitby, B. (1988) AI A Handbook of Professionalism, Chichester, Ellis Horwood.

Whitby B. (1990) AI and the Law: learning to speak each other's language, in Narayanan, A. and Bennun, M. (eds) (1991) op.cit.

Williams, B. (1972) Morality, An Introduction to Ethics, Cambridge Unviversity Press.

Winograd, T. (1972), Understanding Natural Language, New York, Academic Press.

Wright, D. (1971), The Psychology of Moral Behaviour, Harmondsworth, Penguin.

Yazdani M. and Narayanan A. (1984) AI: Human Effects, Chichester, Ellis Horwood.

Yazdani, M. (1986) (ed) Artificial Intelligence, London, Chapman and Hall.

Yazdani, M. and Whitby, B.R.(1987) Artificial Intelligence: Building Birds out of Beer Cans, Robotica 5 pp. 89-92.

Yazdani, M and Whitby, B. (1987) Accidental Nuclear War, the Contribution of AI in AI Review 1,3, 1987.

Subject Index

Name Index